The Poetry of Ambrose Bierce - Volume 3

Ambrose Gwinnett Bierce had a diverse literary, military and journalistic career, during which his sardonic view of human nature ensured he was both frequently critical and frequently criticised. As a writer, his work included short stories, fables, editorials and his journalism, which was often controversial owing to his vehemence and acerbic style.

He was born on June 24th 1842 at Horse Cave Creek in Meigs Country, Ohio. His parents were poor and very religious but instilled in the young Bierce an abiding love of language and literature.

A year at the Kentucky Military Institute prepared him for the Civil War and a source of much of his acclaimed writing. Eventually he moved west to San Francisco where he married and began his literary career in earnest. A few years in England saw his work begin to publish in greater quantities.

By 1891 although his marriage had fallen apart he had published 'An Occurrence at Owl Creek' his classic short story. To this he quickly added volumes of poetry and further volumes of stories and essays as well as a thriving career with the Hearst Organisation. In all his reputation was set as one of America's foremost literary creators.

At the age of 71, in 1913 Bierce departed from Washington, D.C., for a tour of the battlefields upon which he had fought during the civil war. He passed through Louisiana and Texas by December and was crossed into Mexico which was in the throes of revolution. He joined Pancho Villa's army as an observer. It was in Chihuahua where he wrote his last known communication dated 26th December 1913, closing with the words "as to me, I leave here tomorrow for an unknown destination" and then vanished without trace in what would become one of the most famous unexplained disappearances in American history.

Index of Contents
The Man Born Blind
The Militiaman
The National Guardsman
The Naval Constructor
The New Decalogue
The New Enoch
The New 'Ulalume'
The Night Of Election
The Oakland Dog
The Oleomargarine Man
The Opposing Sex
The Passing Of 'Boss' Shepherd
The Passing Show
The Perverted Village After Goldsmith
The Piute
The Politician
The Psoriad
The Pun
The Retrospective Bird
The Rich Testator

The Royal Jester
The Saint And The Monk
The Setting Sachem
The Shafter Shafted
The Spirit Of A Sponge
The Statesmen
The Subdued Editor
The Sunset Gun
The Tables Turned
The Town Of Dae
The Transmigrations Of A Soul
The Unfallen Brave
The Unpardonable Sin
The Valley Of Dry Bones
The Valley Of The Shadow Of Theft
The Van Nessiad
The Veteran
The 'Viduate Dame'
The Weather Wight
The Wise And Good
The Woful Tale Of Mr. Peters
The Woman And The Devil
The Yearly Lie
Thersites
Three Kinds Of A Rogue
Tidings Of Good
Tinker Dick
To A Censor
To A Critic Of Tennyson
To A Dejected Poet
To A Professional Eulogist
To A Stray Dog
To A Summer Poet
To A Word-Warrior
To An Aspirant
To An Insolent Attorney
To 'Colonel' Dan. Burns
To E.S. Salomon
To Either
To Her
To Maude
To My Laundress
To My Liars
To Nanine
To One Across The Way
To One Detested
To Oscar Wilde
To The Bartholdi Statue
To The Fool-Killer
To The Happy Hunting Grounds
To-Day

Twin Unworthies
Two Methods
Two Rogues
Two Shows
Two Statesmen
Unarmed
Uncoloneled
Unexpounded
Vanished At Cock-Crow
Vice Versa
Visions Of Sin
Weather
With a Book
With Mine Own Petard
Woman In Politics
Y'e Foe To Cathaye
Ye Idyll Of Ye Hippopopotamus Quintessence.
Yorick
Aspirants Three
Metempsychosis
'Peaceable Expulsion'
Slander
Slickens
Thanksgiving
The Birth Of The Rail
The Brothers
The Mummery
The Scurril Press
Ambrose Bierce - A Short Biography

The Man Born Blind
A man born blind received his sight
By a painful operation;
And these are things he saw in the light
Of an infant observation.
He saw a merchant, good and wise.
And greatly, too, respected,
Who looked, to those imperfect eyes,
Like a swindler undetected.
He saw a patriot address
A noisy public meeting.
And said: 'Why, that's a calf. I guess.
That for the teat is bleating.'
A doctor stood beside a bed
And shook his summit sadly.
'O see that foul assassin!' said
The man who saw so badly.
He saw a lawyer pleading for

A thief whom they'd been jailing,
And said: 'That's an accomplice, or
My sight again is failing.'
Upon the Bench a Justice sat,
With nothing to restrain him;
''Tis strange,' said the observer, 'that
They ventured to unchain him.'
With theologic works supplied,
He saw a solemn preacher;
'A burglar with his kit,' he cried,
'To rob a fellow creature.'
A bluff old farmer next he saw
Sell produce in a village,
And said: 'What, what! is there no law
To punish men for pillage?'
A dame, tall, fair and stately, passed,
Who many charms united;
He thanked his stars his lot was cast
Where sepulchers were whited.
He saw a soldier stiff and stern,
'Full of strange oaths' and toddy;
But was unable to discern
A wound upon his body.
Ten square leagues of rolling ground
To one great man belonging,
Looked like one little grassy mound
With worms beneath it thronging.
A palace's well-carven stones,
Where Dives dwelt contented,
Seemed built throughout of human bones
With human blood cemented.
He watched the yellow shining thread
A silk-worm was a-spinning;
'That creature's coining gold.' he said,
'To pay some girl for sinning.'
His eyes were so untrained and dim
All politics, religions,
Arts, sciences, appeared to him
But modes of plucking pigeons.
And so he drew his final breath,
And thought he saw with sorrow
Some persons weeping for his death
Who'd be all smiles to-morrow.

The Militiaman

'O warrior with the burnished arms
With bullion cord and tassel
Pray tell me of the lurid charms
Of service and the fierce alarms:

The storming of the castle,
The charge across the smoking field,
The rifles' busy rattle
What thoughts inspire the men who wield
The blade - their gallant souls how steeled
And fortified in battle.'
'Nay, man of peace, seek not to know
War's baleful fascination
The soldier's hunger for the foe,
His dread of safety, joy to go
To court annihilation.
Though calling bugles blow not now,
Nor drums begin to beat yet,
One fear unmans me, I'll allow,
And poisons all my pleasure: How
If I should get my feet wet!'

The National Guardsman
I'm a gorgeous golden hero
And my trade is taking life.
Hear the twittle-twittle-tweero
Of my sibillating fife
And the rub-a-dub-a-dum
Of my big bass drum!
I'm an escort strong and bold,
The Grand Army to protect.
My countenance is cold
And my attitude erect.
I'm a Californian Guard
And my banner flies aloft,
But the stones are O, so hard!
And my feet are O, so soft!

The Naval Constructor
He looked upon the ships as they
All idly lay at anchor,
Their sides with gorgeous workmen gay
The riveter and planker
Republicans and Democrats,
Statesmen and politicians.
He saw the swarm of prudent rats
Swimming for land positions.
He marked each 'belted cruiser' fine,
Her poddy life-belts floating
In tether where the hungry brine
Impinged upon her coating.
He noted with a proud regard,

As any of his class would,
The poplar mast and poplar yard
Above the hull of bass-wood.
He saw the Eastlake frigate tall,
With quaintly carven gable,
Hip-roof and dormer-window-all
With ivy formidable.
In short, he saw our country's hope
In best of all conditions
Equipped, to the last spar and rope,
By working politicians.
He boarded then the noblest ship
And from the harbor glided.
'Adieu, adieu!' fell from his lip.
Verdict: 'He suicided.'

The New Decalogue

Have but one God: thy knees were sore
If bent in prayer to three or four.
Adore no images save those
The coinage of thy country shows.
Take not the Name in vain. Direct
Thy swearing unto some effect.
Thy hand from Sunday work be held
Work not at all unless compelled.
Honor thy parents, and perchance
Their wills thy fortunes may advance.
Kill not - death liberates thy foe
From persecution's constant woe.
Kiss not thy neighbor's wife. Of course
There's no objection to divorce.
To steal were folly, for 'tis plain
In cheating there is greater pain.
Bear not false witness. Shake your head
And say that you have 'heard it said.'
Who stays to covet ne'er will catch
An opportunity to snatch.

The New Enoch

Enoch Arden was an able
Seaman; hear of his mishap
Not in wild mendacious fable,
As 't was told by t' other chap;
For I hold it is a youthful
Indiscretion to tell lies,
And the writer that is truthful
Has the reader that is wise.

Enoch Arden, able seaman,
On an isle was cast away,
And before he was a freeman
Time had touched him up with gray.
Long he searched the fair horizon,
Seated on a mountain top;
Vessel ne'er he set his eyes on
That would undertake to stop.
Seeing that his sight was growing
Dim and dimmer, day by day,
Enoch said he must be going.
So he rose and went away
Went away and so continued
Till he lost his lonely isle:
Mr. Arden was so sinewed
He could row for many a mile.
Compass he had not, nor sextant,
To direct him o'er the sea:
Ere 't was known that he was extant,
At his widow's home was he.
When he saw the hills and hollows
And the streets he could but know,
He gave utterance as follows
To the sentiments below:
'Blast my tarry toplights! (shiver,
Too, my timbers!) but, I say,
W'at a larruk to diskiver,
I have lost me blessid way!
'W'at, alas, would be my bloomin'
Fate if Philip now I see,
Which I lammed? or my old 'oman,
Which has frequent basted me?'
Scenes of childhood swam around him
At the thought of such a lot:
In a swoon his Annie found him
And conveyed him to her cot.
'T was the very house, the garden,
Where their honeymoon was passed:
'T was the place where Mrs. Arden
Would have mourned him to the last.
Ah, what grief she'd known without him!
Now what tears of joy she shed!
Enoch Arden looked about him:
'Shanghaied!' that was all he said.

The New 'Ulalume'
The skies they were ashen and sober,
The leaves they were crisped and sere,
"withering"

It was night in the lonesome October
Of my most immemorial year;
It was hard by the dim lake of Auber,
"down, dark tarn"
In the misty mid region of Weir,
"ghoul-haunted woodland"

The Night Of Election
'O venerable patriot, I pray
Stand not here coatless; at the break of day
We'll know the grand result and even now
The eastern sky is faintly touched with gray.
'It ill befits thine age's hoary crown
This rude environment of rogue and clown,
Who, as the lying bulletins appear,
With drunken cries incarnadine the town.
'But if with noble zeal you stay to note
The outcome of your patriotic vote
For Blaine, or Cleveland, and your native land,
Take - and God bless you! take my overcoat.'
'Done, pard - and mighty white of you. And now
guess the country'll keep the trail somehow.
I aint allowed to vote, the Warden said,
But whacked my coat up on old Stanislow.'

The Oakland Dog
I lay one happy night in bed
And dreamed that all the dogs were dead.
They'd all been taken out and shot
Their bodies strewed each vacant lot.
O'er all the earth, from Berkeley down
To San Leandro's ancient town,
And out in space as far as Niles
I saw their mortal parts in piles.
One stack upreared its ridge so high
Against the azure of the sky
That some good soul, with pious views,
Put up a steeple and sold pews.
No wagging tail the scene relieved:
I never in my life conceived
(I swear it on the Decalogue!)
Such penury of living dog.
The barking and the howling stilled,
The snarling with the snarler killed,
All nature seemed to hold its breath:
The silence was as deep as death.
True, candidates were all in roar

On every platform, as before;
And villains, as before, felt free
To finger the calliope.
True, the Salvationist by night,
And milkman in the early light,
The lonely flutist and the mill
Performed their functions with a will.
True, church bells on a Sunday rang
The sick man's curtain down - the bang
Of trains, contesting for the track,
Out of the shadow called him back.
True, cocks, at all unheavenly hours,
Crew with excruciating powers,
Cats on the woodshed rang and roared,
Fat citizens and fog-horns snored.
But this was all too fine for ears
Accustomed, through the awful years,
To the nocturnal monologues
And day debates of Oakland dogs.
And so the world was silent. Now
What else befell - to whom and how?
Imprimis, then, there were no fleas,
And days of worth brought nights of ease.
Men walked about without the dread
Of being torn to many a shred,
Each fragment holding half a cruse
Of hydrophobia's quickening juice.
They had not to propitiate
Some curst kioodle at each gate,
But entered one another's grounds,
Unscared, and were not fed to hounds.
Women could drive and not a pup
Would lift the horse's tendons up
And let them go - to interject
A certain musical effect.
Even children's ponies went about,
All grave and sober-paced, without
A bulldog hanging to each nose
Proud of his fragrance, I suppose.
Dog being dead, Man's lawless flame
Burned out: he granted Woman's claim,
Children's and those of country, art
all took lodgings in his heart.
When memories of his former shame
Crimsoned his cheeks with sudden flame
He said; 'I know my fault too well
They fawned upon me and I fell.'
Ah! 'twas a lovely world! no more
I met that indisposing bore,
The unseraphic cynogogue
The man who's proud to love a dog.

Thus in my dream the golden reign
Of Reason filled the world again,
And all mankind confessed her sway,
From Walnut Creek to San Jose.

The Oleomargarine Man

Once - in the county of Marin,
Where milk is sold to purchase gin
Renowned for butter and renowned
For fourteen ounces to the pound
A bull stood watching every turn
Of Mr. Wilson with a churn,
As that deigning worthy stalked
About him, eying as he walked,
El Toro's sleek and silken hide,
His neck, his flank and all beside;
Thinking with secret joy: 'I'll spread
That mammal on a slice of bread!'
Soon Mr. Wilson's keen concern
To get the creature in his churn
Unhorsed his caution - made him blind
To the fell vigor of bullkind,
Till, filled with valor to the teeth,
He drew his dasher from its sheath
And bravely brandished it; the while
He smiled a dark, portentous smile;
A deep, sepulchral smile; a wide
And open smile, which, at his side,
The churn to copy vainly tried;
A smile so like the dawn of doom
That all the field was palled in gloom,
And all the trees within a mile,
As tribute to that awful smile,
Made haste, with loyalty discreet,
To fling their shadows at his feet.
Then rose his battle-cry: 'I'll spread
That mammal on a slice of bread!'
To such a night the day had turned
That Taurus dimly was discerned.
He wore so meek and grave an air
It seemed as if, engaged in prayer
This thunderbolt incarnate had
No thought of anything that's bad:
This concentrated earthquake stood
And gave his mind to being good.
Lightly and low he drew his breath
This magazine of sudden death!
All this the thrifty Wilson's glance
Took in, and, crying, 'Now's my chance!'

Upon the bull he sprang amain
To put him in his churn. Again
Rang out his battle-yell: 'I'll spread
That mammal on a slice of bread!'
Sing, Muse, that battle-royal-sing
The deeds that made the region ring,
The blows, the bellowing, the cries,
The dust that darkened all the skies,
The thunders of the contest, all
Nay, none of these things did befall.
A yell there was a rush no more:
El Toro, tranquil as before,
Still stood there basking in the sun,
Nor of his legs had shifted one
Stood there and conjured up his cud
And meekly munched it. Scenes of blood
Had little charm for him. His head
He merely nodded as he said:
'I've spread that butterman upon
A slice of Southern Oregon.'

The Opposing Sex
The Widows of Ashur
Are loud in their wailing:
'No longer the 'masher'
Sees Widows of Ashur!'
So each is a lasher
Of Man's smallest failing.
The Widows of Ashur
Are loud in their wailing.
The Cave of Adullam,
That home of reviling
No wooing can gull 'em
In Cave of Adullam.
No angel can lull 'em
To cease their defiling
The Cave of Adullam,
That home of reviling.
At men they are cursing
The Widows of Ashur;
Themselves, too, for nursing
The men they are cursing.
The praise they're rehearsing
Of every slasher
At men. They are cursing
The Widows of Ashur.

The Passing Of 'Boss' Shepherd

The sullen church-bell's intermittent moan,
The dirge's melancholy monotone,
The measured march, the drooping flags, attest
A great man's progress to his place of rest.
Along broad avenues himself decreed
To serve his fellow men's disputed need
Past parks he raped away from robbers' thrift
And gave to poverty, wherein to lift
Its voice to curse the giver and the gift
Past noble structures that he reared for men
To meet in and revile him, tongue and pen,
Draws the long retinue of death to show
The fit credentials of a proper woe.
'Boss' Shepherd, you are dead. Your hand no more
Throws largess to the mobs that ramp and roar
For blood of benefactors who disdain
Their purity of purpose to explain,
Their righteous motive and their scorn of gain.
Your period of dream - 'twas but a breath
Is closed in the indifference of death.
Sealed in your silences, to you alike
If hands are lifted to applaud or strike.
No more to your dull, inattentive ear
Praise of to-day than curse of yesteryear.
From the same lips the honied phrases fall
That still are bitter from cascades of gall.
We note the shame; you in your depth of dark
The red-writ testimony cannot mark
On every honest cheek; your senses all
Locked, incommunicado, in your pall,
Know not who sit and blush, who stand and bawl.
'Seven Grecian cities claim great Homer dead,
Through which the living Homer begged his bread.'
So sang, as if the thought had been his own,
An unknown bard, improving on a known.
'Neglected genius!' that is sad indeed,
But malice better would ignore than heed,
And Shepherd's soul, we rightly may suspect,
Prayed often for the mercy of neglect
When hardly did he dare to leave his door
Without a guard behind him and before
To save him from the gentlemen that now
In cheap and easy reparation bow
Their corrigible heads above his corse
To counterfeit a grief that's half remorse.
The pageant passes and the exile sleeps,
And well his tongue the solemn secret keeps
Of the great peace he found afar, until,
Death's writ of extradition to fulfill,
They brought him, helpless, from that friendly zone

To be a show and pastime in his own
A final opportunity to those
Who fling with equal aim the stone and rose;
That at the living till his soul is freed,
This at the body to conceal the deed!
Lone on his hill he's lying to await
What added honors may befit his state
The monument, the statue, or the arch
(Where knaves may come to weep and dupes to march)
Builded by clowns to brutalize the scenes
His genius beautified. To get the means,
His newly good traducers all are dunned
For contributions to the conscience fund.
If each subscribe (and pay) one cent 'twill rear
A structure taller than their tallest ear.

The Passing Show

I
I know not if it was a dream. I viewed
A city where the restless multitude,
Between the eastern and the western deep
Had reared gigantic fabrics, strong and rude.
Colossal palaces crowned every height;
Towers from valleys climbed into the light;
O'er dwellings at their feet, great golden domes
Hung in the blue, barbarically bright.
But now, new-glimmering to-east, the day
Touched the black masses with a grace of gray,
Dim spires of temples to the nation's God
Studding high spaces of the wide survey.
Well did the roofs their solemn secret keep
Of life and death stayed by the truce of sleep,
Yet whispered of an hour when sleepers wake,
The fool to hope afresh, the wise to weep.
The gardens greened upon the builded hills
Above the tethered thunders of the mills
With sleeping wheels unstirred to service yet
By the tamed torrents and the quickened rills.
A hewn acclivity, reprieved a space,
Looked on the builder's blocks about his base
And bared his wounded breast in sign to say:
'Strike! 'tis my destiny to lodge your race.
"Twas but a breath ago the mammoth browsed
Upon my slopes, and in my caves I housed
Your shaggy fathers in their nakedness,
While on their foemen's offal they caroused.'
Ships from afar afforested the bay.
Within their huge and chambered bodies lay

The wealth of continents; and merrily sailed
The hardy argosies to far Cathay.
Beside the city of the living spread
Strange fellowship! the city of the dead;
And much I wondered what its humble folk,
To see how bravely they were housed, had said.
Noting how firm their habitations stood,
Broad-based and free of perishable wood
How deep in granite and how high in brass
The names were wrought of eminent and good,
I said: 'When gold or power is their aim,
The smile of beauty or the wage of shame,
Men dwell in cities; to this place they fare
When they would conquer an abiding fame.'
From the red East the sun - a solemn rite
Crowned with a flame the cross upon a height
Above the dead; and then with all his strength
Struck the great city all aroar with light!

II

I know not if it was a dream. I came
Unto a land where something seemed the same
That I had known as 'twere but yesterday,
But what it was I could not rightly name.
It was a strange and melancholy land,
Silent and desolate. On either hand
Lay waters of a sea that seemed as dead,
And dead above it seemed the hills to stand.
Grayed all with age, those lonely hills - ah me,
How worn and weary they appeared to be!
Between their feet long dusty fissures clove
The plain in aimless windings to the sea.
One hill there was which, parted from the rest,
Stood where the eastern water curved a-west.
Silent and passionless it stood. I thought
I saw a scar upon its giant breast.
The sun with sullen and portentous gleam
Hung like a menace on the sea's extreme;
Nor the dead waters, nor the far, bleak bars
Of cloud were conscious of his failing beam.
It was a dismal and a dreadful sight,
That desert in its cold, uncanny light;
No soul but I alone to mark the fear
And imminence of everlasting night!
All presages and prophecies of doom
Glimmered and babbled in the ghastly gloom,
And in the midst of that accursèd scene
A wolf sat howling on a broken tomb.

The Perverted Village After Goldsmith
Sweet Auburn! liveliest village of the plain,
Where Health and Slander welcome every train,
Whence smiling innocence, its tribute paid,
Retires in terror, wounded and dismayed
Dear lovely bowers of gossip and disease,
Whose climate cures us that thy dames may tease,
How often have I knelt upon thy green
And prayed for death, to mitigate their spleen!
How often have I paused on every charm
With mingled admiration and alarm
The brook that runs by many a scandal-mill,
The church whose pastor groans upon the grill,
The cowthorn bush with seats beneath the shade,
Where hearts are struck and reputations flayed;
How often wished thine idle wives, some day,
Might more at whist, less at the devil, play.
Unblest retirement! ere my life's decline
(Killed by detraction) may I witness thine.
How happy she who, shunning shades like these,
Finds in a wolf-den greater peace and ease;
Who quits the place whence truth did earlier fly,
And rather than come back prefers to die!
For her no jealous maids renounce their sleep,
Contriving malices to make her weep;
No iron-faced dames her character debate
And spurn imploring mercy from the gate;
But down she lies to a more peaceful end,
For wolves do not calumniate, but rend
Sinks piecemeal to their maws, a willing prey,
While resignation lubricates the way,
And all her prospects brighten at the last:
To wolves, not women, an approved repast.

The Piute
Unbeautiful is the Piute!
Howe'er bedecked with bravery,
His person is unsavory
Of soap he's destitute.
He multiplies upon the earth
In spite of all admonishing;
All censure his astonishing
And versatile unworth.
Upon the Reservation wide
We give for his inhabiting
He goes a-jackass rabbiting
To furnish his inside.
The hopper singing in the grass
He seizes with avidity:

He loves its tart acidity,
And gobbles all that pass.
He penetrates the spider's veil,
Industriously pillages
The toads' defenseless villages,
And shadows home the snail.
He lightly runs to earth the quaint
Red worm and, deftly troweling,
He makes it with his boweling
Familiarly acquaint.
He tracks the pine-nut to its lair,
Surrounds it with celerity,
Regards it with asperity
Smiles, and it isn't there!
I wish he'd open up a grin
Of adequate vivacity
And carrying capacity
To take his Agent in.

The Politician

'Let Glory's sons manipulate
The tiller of the Ship of State.
Be mine the humble, useful toil
To work the tiller of the soil.'

The Psoriad

The King of Scotland, years and years ago,
Convened his courtiers in a gallant row
And thus addressed them:
'Gentle sirs, from you
Abundant counsel I have had, and true:
What laws to make to serve the public weal;
What laws of Nature's making to repeal;
What old religion is the only true one,
And what the greater merit of some new one;
What friends of yours my favor have forgot;
Which of your enemies against me plot.
In harvests ample to augment my treasures,
Behold the fruits of your sagacious measures!
The punctual planets, to their periods just,
Attest your wisdom and approve my trust.
Lo! the reward your shining virtues bring:
The grateful placemen bless their useful king!
But while you quaff the nectar of my favor
I mean somewhat to modify its flavor
By just infusing a peculiar dash
Of tonic bitter in the calabash.

And should you, too abstemious, disdain it,
Egad! I'll hold your noses till you drain it!
'You know, you dogs, your master long has felt
A keen distemper in the royal pelt
A testy, superficial irritation,
Brought home, I fancy, from some foreign nation.
For this a thousand simples you've prescribed
Unguents external, draughts to be imbibed.
You've plundered Scotland of its plants, the seas
You've ravished, and despoiled the Hebrides,
To brew me remedies which, in probation,
Were sovereign only in their application.
In vain, and eke in pain, have I applied
Your flattering unctions to my soul and hide:
Physic and hope have been my daily food
I've swallowed treacle by the holy rood!
'Your wisdom, which sufficed to guide the year
And tame the seasons in their mad career,
When set to higher purposes has failed me
And added anguish to the ills that ailed me.
Nor that alone, but each ambitious leech
His rivals' skill has labored to impeach
By hints equivocal in secret speech.
For years, to conquer our respective broils,
We've plied each other with pacific oils.
In vain: your turbulence is unallayed,
My flame unquenched; your rioting unstayed;
My life so wretched from your strife to save it
That death were welcome did I dare to brave it.
With zeal inspired by your intemperate pranks,
My subjects muster in contending ranks.
Those fling their banners to the startled breeze
To champion some royal ointment; these
The standard of some royal purge display
And 'neath that ensign wage a wasteful fray!
Brave tongues are thundering from sea to sea,
Torrents of sweat roll reeking o'er the lea!
My people perish in their martial fear,
And rival bagpipes cleave the royal ear!
'Now, caitiffs, tremble, for this very hour
Your injured sovereign shall assert his power!
Behold this lotion, carefully compound
Of all the poisons you for me have found
Of biting washes such as tan the skin,
And drastic drinks to vex the parts within.
What aggravates an ailment will produce
I mean to rub you with this dreadful juice!
Divided counsels you no more shall hatch
At last you shall unanimously scratch.
Kneel, villains, kneel, and doff your shirts - God bless us!
They'll seem, when you resume them, robes of Nessus!'

The sovereign ceased, and, sealing what he spoke,
From Arthur's Seat confirming thunders broke.
The conscious culprits, to their fate resigned,
Sank to their knees, all piously inclined.
This act, from high Ben Lomond where she floats,
The thrifty goddess, Caledonia, notes.
Glibly as nimble sixpence, down she tilts
Headlong, and ravishes away their kilts,
Tears off each plaid and all their shirts discloses,
Removes each shirt and their broad backs exposes.
The king advanced - then cursing fled amain
Dashing the phial to the stony plain
(Where't straight became a fountain brimming o'er,
Whence Father Tweed derives his liquid store)
For lo! already on each back sans stitch
The red sign manual of the Rosy Witch!

The Pun

Hail, peerless Pun! thou last and best,
Most rare and excellent bequest
Of dying idiot to the wit
He died of, rat - like, in a pit!
Thyself disguised, in many a way
Thou let'st thy sudden splendor play,
Adorning all where'er it turns,
As the revealing bull's-eye burns,
Of the dim thief, and plays its trick
Upon the lock he means to pick.
Yet sometimes, too, thou dost appear
As boldly as a brigadier
Tricked out with marks and signs, all o'er,
Of rank, brigade, division, corps,
To show by every means he can
An officer is not a man;
Or naked, with a lordly swagger,
Proud as a cur without a wagger,
Who says: 'See simple worth prevail
All dog, sir - not a bit of tail!'
'T is then men give thee loudest welcome,
As if thou wert a soul from Hell come.
O obvious Pun! thou hast the grace
Of skeleton clock without a case
With all its boweling displayed,
And all its organs on parade.
Dear Pun, you're common ground of bliss,
Where Punch and I can meet and kiss;
Than thee my wit can stoop no low'r
No higher his does ever soar.

The Retrospective Bird

His caw is a cackle, his eye is dim,
And he mopes all day on the lowest limb;
Not a word says he, but he snaps his bill
And twitches his palsied head, as a quill,
The ultimate plume of his pride and hope,
Quits his now featherless nose-of-the-Pope,
Leaving that eminence brown and bare
Exposed to the Prince of the Power of the Air.
And he sits and he thinks: 'I'm an old, old man,
Mateless and chickless, the last of my clan,
But I'd give the half of the days gone by
To perch once more on the branches high,
And hear my great-grand-daddy's comical croaks
In authorized versions of Bulletin jokes.'

The Rich Testator

He lay on his bed and solemnly 'signed,'
Gasping - perhaps 'twas a jest he meant:
'This of a sound and disposing mind
Is the last ill-will and contestament.'

The Royal Jester

Once on a time, so ancient poets sing,
There reigned in Godknowswhere a certain king.
So great a monarch ne'er before was seen:
He was a hero, even to his queen,
In whose respect he held so high a place
That none was higher, nay, not even the ace.
He was so just his Parliament declared
Those subjects happy whom his laws had spared;
So wise that none of the debating throng
Had ever lived to prove him in the wrong;
So good that Crime his anger never feared,
And Beauty boldly plucked him by the beard;
So brave that if his army got a beating
None dared to face him when he was retreating.
This monarch kept a Fool to make his mirth,
And loved him tenderly despite his worth.
Prompted by what caprice I cannot say,
He called the Fool before the throne one day
And to that jester seriously said:
'I'll abdicate, and you shall reign instead,
While I, attired in motley, will make sport
To entertain your Majesty and Court.'

'T was done and the Fool governed. He decreed
The time of harvest and the time of seed;
Ordered the rains and made the weather clear,
And had a famine every second year;
Altered the calendar to suit his freak,
Ordaining six whole holidays a week;
Religious creeds and sacred books prepared;
Made war when angry and made peace when scared.
New taxes he inspired; new laws he made;
Drowned those who broke them, who observed them, flayed,
In short, he ruled so well that all who'd not
Been starved, decapitated, hanged or shot
Made the whole country with his praises ring,
Declaring he was every inch a king;
And the High Priest averred 't was very odd
If one so competent were not a god.
Meantime, his master, now in motley clad,
Wore such a visage, woeful, wan and sad,
That some condoled with him as with a brother
Who, having lost a wife, had got another.
Others, mistaking his profession, often
Approached him to be measured for a coffin.
For years this highborn jester never broke
The silence - he was pondering a joke.
At last, one day, in cap - and bells arrayed,
He strode into the Council and displayed
A long, bright smile, that glittered in the gloom
Like a gilt epithet within a tomb.
Posing his bauble like a leader's staff,
To give the signal when (and why) to laugh,
He brought it down with peremptory stroke
And simultaneously cracked his joke!
I can't repeat it, friends. I ne'er could school
Myself to quote from any other fool:
A jest, if it were worse than mine, would start
My tears; if better, it would break my heart.
So, if you please, I'll hold you but to state
That royal Jester's melancholy fate.
The insulted nation, so the story goes,
Rose as one man - the very dead arose,
Springing indignant from the riven tomb,
And babes unborn leapt swearing from the womb!
All to the Council Chamber clamoring went,
By rage distracted and on vengeance bent.
In that vast hall, in due disorder laid,
The tools of legislation were displayed,
And the wild populace, its wrath to sate,
Seized them and heaved them at the Jester's pate.
Mountains of writing paper; pools and seas
Of ink, awaiting, to become decrees,
Royal approval - and the same in stacks

Lay ready for attachment, backed with wax;
Pens to make laws, erasers to amend them;
With mucilage convenient to extend them;
Scissors for limiting their application,
And acids to repeal all legislation
These, flung as missiles till the air was dense,
Were most offensive weapons of offense,
And by their aid the Fool was nigh destroyed.
They ne'er had been so harmlessly employed.
Whelmed underneath a load of legal cap,
His mouth egurgitating ink on tap,
His eyelids mucilaginously sealed,
His fertile head by scissors made to yield
Abundant harvestage of ears, his pelt,
In every wrinkle and on every welt,
Quickset with pencil-points from feet to gills
And thickly studded with a pride of quills,
The royal Jester in the dreadful strife
Was made (in short) an editor for life!
An idle tale, and yet a moral lurks
In this as plainly as in greater works.
I shall not give it birth: one moral here
Would die of loneliness within a year.

The Saint And The Monk
Saint Peter at the gate of Heaven displayed
The tools and terrors of his awful trade;
The key, the frown as pitiless as night,
That slays intending trespassers at sight,
And, at his side in easy reach, the curled
Interrogation points all ready to be hurled.
Straight up the shining cloudway (it so chanced
No others were about) a soul advanced
A fat, orbicular and jolly soul
With laughter-lines upon each rosy jowl
A monk so prepossessing that the saint
Admired him, breathless, until weak and faint,
Forgot his frown and all his questions too,
Forgoing even the customary 'Who?'
Threw wide the gate and, with a friendly grin,
Said, ''Tis a very humble home, but pray walk in.'
The soul smiled pleasantly. 'Excuse me, please
Who's in there?' By insensible degrees
The impudence dispelled the saint's esteem,
As growing snores annihilate a dream.
The frown began to blacken on his brow,
His hand to reach for 'Whence?' and 'Why?' and 'How?'
'O, no offense, I hope,' the soul explained;
'I'm rather - well, particular. I've strained

A point in coming here at all; 'tis said
That Susan Anthony (I hear she's dead
At last) and all her followers are here.
As company, they'd be - confess it - rather queer.'
The saint replied, his rising anger past:
'What can I do? - the law is hard-and-fast,
Albeit unwritten and on earth unknown
An oral order issued from the Throne.
By but one sin has Woman e'er incurred
God's wrath. To accuse Them Loud of that would be absurd.'
That friar sighed, but, calling up a smile,
Said, slowly turning on his heel the while:
'Farewell, my friend. Put up the chain and bar
I'm going, so please you, where the pretty women are.'

The Setting Sachem
'Twas an Injin chieftain, in feathers all fine,
Who stood on the ocean's rim;
There were numberless leagues of excellent brine
But there wasn't enough for him.
So he knuckled a thumb in his painted eye,
And added a tear to the scant supply.
The surges were breaking with thund'rous voice,
The winds were a-shrieking shrill;
This warrior thought that a trifle of noise
Was needed to fill the bill.
So he lifted the top of his head off and scowled
Exalted his voice, did this chieftain, and howled!
The sun was aflame in a field of gold
That hung o'er the Western Sea;
Bright banners of light were broadly unrolled,
As banners of light should be.
But no one was 'speaking a piece' to that sun,
And therefore this Medicine Man begun:
'O much heap of bright! O big ball of warm!
I've tracked you from sea to sea!
For the Paleface has been at some pains to inform
Me, you are the emblem of me.
He says to me, cheerfully: 'Westward Ho!'
And westward I've hoed a most difficult row.
'Since you are the emblem of me, I presume
That I am the emblem of you,
And thus, as we're equals, 't is safe to assume,
That one great law governs us two.
So now if I set in the ocean with thee,
With thee I shall rise again out of the sea.'
His eloquence first, and his logic the last!
Such orators die! - and he died:
The trump was against him - his luck bad - he 'passed'

And so he 'passed out' - with the tide.
This Injin is rid of the world with a whim
The world it is rid of his speeches and him.

The Shafter Shafted
Well, James McMillan Shafter, you're a Judge
At least you were when last I knew of you;
And if the people since have made you budge
I did not notice it. I've much to do
Without endeavoring to follow, through
The miserable squabbles, dust and smudge,
The fate of even the veteran contenders
Who fight with flying colors and suspenders.
Being a Judge, 'tis natural and wrong
That you should villify the public press
Save while you are a candidate. That song
Is easy quite to sing, and I confess
It wins applause from hearers who have less
Of spiritual graces than belong
To audiences of another kidney
Men, for example, like Sir Philip Sidney.
Newspapers, so you say, don't always treat
The Judges with respect. That may be so
And still no harm done, for I swear I'll eat
My legs and in the long hereafter go,
Snake-like, upon my belly if you'll show
All Judges are respectable and sweet.
For some of them are rogues and the world's laughter's
Directed at some others, for they're Shafters.

The Spirit Of A Sponge
I dreamed one night that Stephen Massett died,
And for admission up at Heaven applied.
'Who are you?' asked St. Peter. Massett said:
'Jeems Pipes, of Pipesville.' Peter bowed his head,
Opened the gates and said: 'I'm glad to know you,
And wish we'd something better, sir, to show you.'
'Don't mention it,' said Stephen, looking bland,
And was about to enter, hat in hand,
When from a cloud below such fumes arose
As tickled tenderly his conscious nose.
He paused, replaced his hat upon his head,
Turned back and to the saintly warden said,
O'er his already sprouting wings: 'I swear
I smell some broiling going on down there!'
So Massett's paunch, attracted by the smell,
Followed his nose and found a place in Hell.

The Statesmen
How blest the land that counts among
Her sons so many good and wise,
To execute great feats of tongue
When troubles rise.
Behold them mounting every stump
Our liberty by speech to guard.
Observe their courage: see them jump
And come down hard!
'Walk up, walk up!' each cries aloud,
'And learn from me what you must do
To turn aside the thunder cloud,
The earthquake too.
'Beware the wiles of yonder quack
Who stuffs the ears of all that pass.
I-I alone can show that black
Is white as grass.'
They shout through all the day and break
The silence of the night as well.
They'd make - I wish they'd go and make
Of Heaven a Hell.
A advocates free silver, B
Free trade and C free banking laws.
Free board, clothes, lodging would from me
Win warm applause.
Lo, D lifts up his voice: 'You see
The single tax on land would fall
On all alike.' More evenly
No tax at all.
'With paper money' bellows E
'We'll all be rich as lords.' No doubt
And richest of the lot will be
The chap without.
As many 'cures' as addle wits
Who know not what the ailment is!
Meanwhile the patient foams and spits
Like a gin fizz.
Alas, poor Body Politic,
Your fate is all too clearly read:
To be not altogether quick,
Nor very dead.
You take your exercise in squirms,
Your rest in fainting fits between.
'T is plain that your disorder's worms
Worms fat and lean.
Worm Capital, Worm Labor dwell
Within your maw and muscle's scope.
Their quarrels make your life a Hell,

Your death a hope.
God send you find not such an end
To ills however sharp and huge!
God send you convalesce! God send
You vermifuge.

The Subdued Editor

Pope-choker Pixley sat in his den
A-chewin' upon his quid.
He thought it was Leo Thirteen, and then
He bit it intenser, he did.
The amber which overflew from the cud
Like rivers which burst out of bounds
'Twas peculiar grateful to think it blood
A-gushin' from Papal wounds.
A knockin' was heard uponto the door
Where some one a-waitin' was.
'Come in,' said the shedder of priestly gore,
Arrestin' to once his jaws.
The person which entered was curly of hair
And smilin' as ever you see;
His eyes was blue, and uncommon fair
Was his physiognomee.
And yet there was some'at remarkable grand
And the editor says as he looks:
'Your Height' (it was Highness, you understand,
That he meant, but he spoke like books)
'Your Height, I am in. I'm the editor man
Of this paper - which is to say,
I'm the owner, too, and it's alway ran
In the independentest way!
'Not a damgaloot can interfere,
A-shapin' my course for me:
This paper's (and nothing can make it veer)
Pixleian in policee!'
'It's little to me,' said the sunny youth,
'If journals is better or worse
Where I am to home they won't keep, in truth,
The climate is that perverse.
'I've come, howsomever, your mind to light
With a more superior fire:
You'll have naught hencefor'ard to do but write,
While I sets by and inspire.
'We'll make it hot all round, bedad!'
And his laughture was loud and free.
'The devil!' cried Pixley, surpassin' mad.
'Exactly, my friend - that's me.'
So he took a chair and a feather fan,
And he sets and sets and sets,

Inspirin' that humbled editor man,
Which sweats and sweats and sweats!
All unavailin' his struggles be,
And it's, O, a weepin' sight
To see a great editor bold and free
Reducted to sech a plight!

The Sunset Gun
Off Santa Cruz the western wave
Was crimson as with blood:
The sun was sinking to his grave
Beneath that angry flood.
Sir Walter Turnbull, brave and stout,
Then shouted, 'Ho! lads; run
The powder and the ball bring out
To fire the sunset gun.
'That punctual orb did ne'er omit
To keep, by land or sea,
Its every engagement; it
Shall never wait for me.'
Behold the black-mouthed cannon stand,
Ready with charge and prime,
The lanyard in the gunner's hand.
Sir Walter waits the time.
The glowing orb sinks in the sea,
And clouds of steam aspire,
Then fade, and the horizon's free.
Sir Walter thunders: 'Fire!'
The gunner pulls - the lanyard parts
And not a sound ensues.
The beating of ten thousand hearts
Was heard at Santa Cruz!
Off Santa Cruz the western wave
Was crimson as with blood;
The sun, with visage stern and grave,
Came back from out the flood.

The Tables Turned
Over the man the street car ran,
And the driver did never grin.
'O killer of men, pray tell me when
Your laughter means to begin.
'Ten years to a day I've observed you slay,
And I never have missed before
Your jubilant peals as your crunching wheels
Were spattered with human gore.
'Why is it, my boy, that you smother your joy,

And why do you make no sign
Of the merry mind that is dancing behind
A solemner face than mine?'
The driver replied: 'I would laugh till I cried
If I had bisected you;
But I'd like to explain, if I can for the pain,
'T is myself that I've cut in two.'

The Town Of Dae
Swains and maidens, young and old,
You to me this tale have told.
Where the squalid town of Dae
Irks the comfortable sea,
Spreading webs to gather fish,
As for wealth we set a wish,
Dwelt a king by right divine,
Sprung from Adam's royal line,
Town of Dae by the sea,
Divers kinds of kings there be.
Name nor fame had Picklepip:
Ne'er a soldier nor a ship
Bore his banners in the sun;
Naught knew he of kingly sport,
And he held his royal court
Under an inverted tun.
Love and roses, ages through,
Bloom where cot and trellis stand;
Never yet these blossoms grew
Never yet was room for two
In a cask upon the strand.
So it happened, as it ought,
That his simple schemes he wrought
Through the lagging summer's day
In a solitary way.
So it happened, as was best,
That he took his nightly rest
With no dreadful incubus
This way eyed and that way tressed,
Featured thus, and thus, and thus,
Lying lead - like on a breast
By cares of State enough oppressed.
Yet in dreams his fancies rude
Claimed a lordly latitude.
Town of Dae by the sea,
Dreamers mate above their state
And waken back to their degree.
Once to cask himself away
He prepared at close of day.
As he tugged with swelling throat

At a most unkingly coat
Not to get it off, but on,
For the serving sun was gone
Passed a silk-appareled sprite
Toward her castle on the height,
Seized and set the garment right.
Turned the startled Picklepip
Splendid crimson cheek and lip!
Turned again to sneak away,
But she bade the villain stay,
Bade him thank her, which he did
With a speech that slipped and slid,
Sprawled and stumbled in its gait
As a dancer tries to skate.
Town of Dae by the sea,
In the face of silk and lace
Rags too bold should never be.
Lady Minnow cocked her head:
'Mister Picklepip,' she said,
'Do you ever think to wed?'
Town of Dae by the sea,
No fair lady ever made a
Wicked speech like that to me!
Wretched little Picklepip
Said he hadn't any ship,
Any flocks at his command,
Nor to feed them any land;
Said he never in his life
Owned a mine to keep a wife.
But the guilty stammer so
That his meaning wouldn't flow;
So he thought his aim to reach
By some figurative speech:
Said his Fate had been unkind
Had pursued him from behind
(How the mischief could it else?)
Came upon him unaware,
Caught him by the collar - there
Gushed the little lady's glee
Like a gush of golden bells:
'Picklepip, why, that is me!'
Town of Dae by the sea,
Grammar's for great scholars - she
Loved the summer and the lea.
Stupid little Picklepip
Allowed the subtle hint to slip
Maundered on about the ship
That he did not chance to own;
Told this grievance o'er and o'er,
Knowing that she knew before;
Told her how he dwelt alone.

Lady Minnow, for reply,
Cut him off with 'So do I!'
But she reddened at the fib;
Servitors had she, ad lib.
Town of Dae by the sea,
In her youth who speaks no truth
Ne'er shall young and honest be.
Witless little Picklepip
Manned again his mental ship
And veered her with a sudden shift.
Painted to the lady's thought
How he wrestled and he wrought
Stoutly with the swimming drift
By the kindly river brought
From the mountain to the sea,
Fuel for the town of Dae.
Tedious tale for lady's ear:
From her castle on the height,
She had watched her water-knight
Through the seasons of a year,
Challenge more than met his view
And conquer better than he knew.
Now she shook her pretty pate
And stamped her foot - 't was growing late:
'Mister Picklepip, when I
Drifting seaward pass you by;
When the waves my forehead kiss
And my tresses float above
Dead and drowned for lack of love
You'll be sorry, sir, for this!'
And the silly creature cried
Feared, perchance, the rising tide.
Town of Dae by the sea,
Madam Adam, when she had 'em,
May have been as bad as she.
Fiat lux! Love's lumination
Fell in floods of revelation!
Blinded brain by world aglare,
Sense of pulses in the air,
Sense of swooning and the beating
Of a voice somewhere repeating
Something indistinctly heard!
And the soul of Picklepip
Sprang upon his trembling lip,
But he spake no further word
Of the wealth he did not own;
In that moment had outgrown
Ship and mine and flock and land
Even his cask upon the strand.
Dropped a stricken star to earth,
Type of wealth and worldly worth.

Clomb the moon into the sky,
Type of love's immensity!
Shaking silver seemed the sea,
Throne of God the town of Dae!
Town of Dae by the sea,
From above there cometh love,
Blessing all good souls that be.

The Transmigrations Of A Soul

What! Pixley, must I hear you call the roll
Of all the vices that infest your soul?
Was't not enough that lately you did bawl
Your money-worship in the ears of all?
Still must you crack your brazen cheek to tell
That though a miser you're a sot as well?
Still must I hear how low your taste has sunk
From getting money down to getting drunk?
Who worships money, damning all beside,
And shows his callous knees with pious pride,
Speaks with half-knowledge, for no man e'er scorns
His own possessions, be they coins or corns.
You've money, neighbor; had you gentle birth
You'd know, as now you never can, its worth.
You've money; learning is beyond your scope,
Deaf to your envy, stubborn to your hope.
But if upon your undeserving head
Science and letters had their glory shed;
If in the cavern of your skull the light
Of knowledge shone where now eternal night
Breeds the blind, poddy, vapor-fatted naughts
Of cerebration that you think are thoughts
Black bats in cold and dismal corners hung
That squeak and gibber when you move your tongue
You would not write, in Avarice's defense,
A senseless eulogy on lack of sense,
Nor show your eagerness to sacrifice
All noble virtues to one loathsome vice.
You've money; if you'd manners too you'd shame
To boast your weakness or your baseness name.
Appraise the things you have, but measure not
The things denied to your unhappy lot.
He values manners lighter than a cork
Who combs his beard at table with a fork.
Hare to seek sin and tortoise to forsake,
The laws of taste condemn you to the stake
To expiate, where all the world may see,
The crime of growing old disgracefully.
Religion, learning, birth and manners, too,
All that distinguishes a man from you,

Pray damn at will: all shining virtues gain
An added luster from a rogue's disdain.
But spare the young that proselyting sin,
A toper's apotheosis of gin.
If not our young, at least our pigs may claim
Exemption from the spectacle of shame!
Are you not he who lately out of shape
Blew a brass trumpet to denounce the grape?
Who led the brave teetotalers afield
And slew your leader underneath your shield?
Swore that no man should drink unless he flung
Himself across your body at the bung?
Who vowed if you'd the power you would fine
The Son of God for making water wine?
All trails to odium you tread and boast,
Yourself enamored of the dirtiest most.
One day to be a miser you aspire,
The next to wallow drunken in the mire;
The third, lo! you're a meritorious liar!
Pray, in the catalogue of all your graces,
Have theft and cowardice no honored places?
Yield thee, great Satan - here's a rival name
With all thy vices and but half thy shame!
Quick to the letter of the precept, quick
To the example of the elder Nick;
With as great talent as was e'er applied
To fool a teacher and to fog a guide;
With slack allegiance and boundless greed,
To paunch the profit of a traitor deed,
He aims to make thy glory all his own,
And crowd his master from the infernal throne!

The Unfallen Brave

Not all in sorrow and in tears,
To pay of gratitude's arrears
The yearly sum
Not prompted, wholly by the pride
Of those for whom their friends have died,
To-day we come.
Another aim we have in view
Than for the buried boys in blue
To dropp a tear:
Memorial Day revives the chin
Of Barnes, and Salomon chimes in
That's why we're here.
And when in after-ages they
Shall pass, like mortal men, away,
Their war-song sung,
Then fame will tell the tale anew

Of how intrepidly they drew
The deadly tongue.
Then cull white lilies for the graves
Of Liberty's loquacious braves,
And roses red.
Those represent their livers, these
The blood that in unmeasured seas
They did not shed.

The Unpardonable Sin
I reckon that ye never knew,
That dandy slugger, Tom Carew,
He had a touch as light an' free
As that of any honey-bee;
But where it lit there wasn't much
To jestify another touch.
O, what a Sunday - school it was
To watch him puttin' up his paws
An' roominate upon their heft
Particular his holy left!
Tom was my style - that's all I say;
Some others may be equal gay.
What's come of him? Dunno, I'm sure
He's dead - which make his fate obscure.
I only started in to clear
One vital p'int in his career,
Which is to say afore he died
He soiled his erming mighty snide.
Ye see he took to politics
And learnt them statesmen-fellers' tricks;
Pulled wires, wore stovepipe hats, used scent,
Just like he was the President;
Went to the Legislator; spoke
Right out agin the British yoke
But that was right. He let his hair
Grow long to qualify for Mayor,
An' once or twice he poked his snoot
In Congress like a low galoot!
It had to come - no gent can hope
To wrastle God agin the rope.
Tom went from bad to wuss. Being dead,
I s'pose it oughtn't to be said,
For sech inikities as flow
From politics ain't fit to know;
But, if you think it's actin' white
To tell it - Thomas throwed a fight!

The Valley Of Dry Bones

With crow bones all the land is white,
From the gates of morn to the gates of night.
Picked clean, they lie on the cumbered ground,
And the politician's paunch is round;
And he strokes it down and across as he sings:
'I've eaten my fill of the legs and wings,
The neck, the back, the pontifical nose,
Breast, belly and gizzard, for everything goes.
The meat that's dark (and there's none that's white)
Exceeded the need of my appetite,
But I've bravely stuck to the needful work
That a hungry domestic hog would shirk.
I've eaten the fowl that the Fates commend
To reluctant lips of the People's Friend.
Rank unspeakably, bitter as gall,
Is the bird, but I've eaten it, feathers and all.
I'm a dutiful statesman, I am, although
I really don't like a diet of crow.
So I've dined all alone in a furtive way,
But my platter I've cleaned every blessed day.
They say that I bolt; so I do - my bird;
They say that I sulk, but they've widely erred!
O Lord! if my enemies only knew
How I'm full to the throat with the corvic stew
They'd open their ears to hear me profess
The faith compelled by the corvic stress,
(For, alas! necessity knows no law)
In the heavenly caucus - 'Caw! Caw! Caw!"
And that ornithanthropical person tried
By flapping his arms on the air to ride;
But I knew by the way that he clacked his bill
He was just the poor, featherless biped, Dave Hill.

The Valley Of The Shadow Of Theft

In fair Yosemite, that den of thieves
Wherein the minions of the moon divide
The travelers' purses, lo! the Devil grieves,
His larger share as leader still denied.
El Capitan, foreseeing that his reign
May be disputed too, beclouds his head.
The joyous Bridal Veil is torn in twain
And the crepe steamer dangles there instead.
The Vernal Fall abates her pleasant speed
And hesitates to take the final plunge,
For rumors reach her that another greed
Awaits her in the Valley of the Sponge.
The Brothers envy the accord of mind
And peace of purpose (by the good deplored

As honor among Commissioners) which bind
That confraternity of crime, the Board.
The Half-Dome bows its riven face to weep,
But not, as formerly, because bereft:
Prophetic dreams afflict him when asleep
Of losing his remaining half by theft.
Ambitious knaves! has not the upper sod
Enough of room for every crime that crawls
But you must loot the Palaces of God
And daub your filthy names upon the walls?

The Van Nessiad
From end to end, thine avenue, Van Ness,
Rang with the cries of battle and distress!
Brave lungs were thundering with dreadful sound
And perspiration smoked along the ground!
Sing, heavenly muse, to ears of mortal clay,
The meaning, cause and finish of the fray.
Great Porter Ashe (invoking first the gods,
Who signed their favor with assenting nods
That snapped off half their heads - their necks grown dry
Since last the nectar cup went circling by)
Resolved to build a stable on his lot,
His neighbors fiercely swearing he should not.
Said he: 'I build that stable!' 'No, you don't,'
Said they. 'I can!' 'You can't!' 'I will!' 'You won't!'
'By heaven!' he swore; 'not only will I build,
But purchase donkeys till the place is filled!'
'Needless expense,' they sneered in tones of ice
'The owner's self, if lodged there, would suffice.'
For three long months the awful war they waged:
With women, women, men with men engaged,
While roaring babes and shrilling poodles raged!
Jove, from Olympus, where he still maintains
His ancient session (with rheumatic pains
Touched by his long exposure) marked the strife,
Interminable but by loss of life;
For malediction soon exhausts the breath
If not, old age itself is certain death.
Lo! he holds high in heaven the fatal beam;
A golden pan depends from each, extreme;
This feels of Porter's fate the downward stress,
That bears the destiny of all Van Ness.
Alas! the rusted scales, their life all gone,
Deliver judgment neither pro nor con:
The dooms hang level and the war goes on.
With a divine, contemptuous disesteem
Jove dropped the pans and kicked, himself, the beam:
Then, to decide the strife, with ready wit,

The nickel that he did not care for it
Twirled absently, remarking: 'See it spin:
Head, Porter loses; tail, the others win.'
The conscious nickel, charged with doom, spun round,
Portentously and made a ringing sound,
Then, staggering beneath its load of fate,
Sank rattling, died at last and lay in state.
Jove scanned the disk and then, as is his wont,
Raised his considering orbs, exclaiming: 'Front!'
With leisurely alacrity approached
The herald god, to whom his mind he broached:
'In San Francisco two belligerent Powers,
Such as contended round great Ilion's towers,
Fight for a stable, though in either class
There's not a horse, and but a single ass.
Achilles Ashe, with formidable jaw
Assails a Trojan band with fierce hee-haw,
Firing the night with brilliant curses. They
With dark vituperation gloom the day.
Fate, against which nor gods nor men compete,
Decrees their victory and his defeat.
With haste, good Mercury, betake thee hence
And salivate him till he has no sense!'
Sheer downward shot the messenger afar,
Trailing a splendor like a falling star!
With dimming lustre through the air he burned,
Vanished, nor till another sun returned.
The sovereign of the gods superior smiled,
Beaming benignant, fatherly and mild:
'Is Destiny's decree performed, my lad?
And has he now no sense?' 'Ah, sire, he never had.'

The Veteran

John Jackson, once a soldier bold,
Hath still a martial feeling;
So, when he sees a foe, behold!
He charges him with stealing.
He cares not how much ground to-day
He gives for men to doubt him;
He's used to giving ground, they say,
Who lately fought with-out him.
When, for the battle to be won,
His gallantry was needed,
They say each time a loaded gun
Went off-so, likewise, he did.
And when discharged (for war's a sport
So hot he had to leave it)
He made a very loud report,
But no one did believe it.

The 'Viduate Dame'

'Tis the widow of Thomas Blythe,
And she goeth upon the spree,
And red are cheeks of the bystanders
For her acts are light and free.
In a seven-ounce costume
The widow of Thomas Blythe,
Perched high on the window ledge,
The difficult can-can tryeth.
Ten constables they essay
To bate the dame's halloing.
With the widow of Thomas Blythe
Their hands are overflowing,
And they cry: 'Call the National Guard
To quell this parlous muss
For all of the widows of Thomas Blythe
Are upon the spree and us!'
O long shall the eerie tale be told
By that posse's surviving tithe;
And with tears bedewed he'll sing this rude
Ballad of the widow of Thomas Blythe.

The Weather Wight

The way was long, the hill was steep,
My footing scarcely I could keep.
The night enshrouded me in gloom,
I heard the ocean's distant boom
The trampling of the surges vast
Was borne upon the rising blast.
'God help the mariner,' I cried,
'Whose ship to-morrow braves the tide!'
Then from the impenetrable dark
A solemn voice made this remark:
'For this locality - warm, bright;
Barometer unchanged; breeze light.'
'Unseen consoler-man,' I cried,
'Whoe'er you are, where'er abide,
'Thanks - but my care is somewhat less
For Jack's, than for my own, distress.
'Could I but find a friendly roof,
Small odds what weather were aloof.
'For he whose comfort is secure
Another's woes can well endure.'
'The latch-string's out,' the voice replied,
'And so's the door - jes' step inside.'
Then through the darkness I discerned

A hovel, into which I turned.
Groping about beneath its thatch,
I struck my head and then a match.
A candle by that gleam betrayed
Soon lent paraffinaceous aid.
A pallid, bald and thin old man
I saw, who this complaint began:
'Through summer suns and winter snows
I sets observin' of my toes.
'I rambles with increasin' pain
The path of duty, but in vain.
'Rewards and honors pass me by
No Congress hears this raven cry!'
Filled with astonishment, I spoke:
'Thou ancient raven, why this croak?
'With observation of your toes
What Congress has to do, Heaven knows!
'And swallow me if e'er I knew
That one could sit and ramble too!'
To answer me that ancient swain
Took up his parable again:
'Through winter snows and summer suns
A Weather Bureau here I runs.
'I calls the turn, and can declare
Jes' when she'll storm and when she'll fair.
'Three times a day I sings out clear
The probs to all which wants to hear.
'Some weather stations run with light
Frivolity is seldom right.
'A scientist from times remote,
In Scienceville my birth is wrote.
'And when I h'ist the 'rainy' sign
Jes' take your clo'es in off the line.'
'Not mine, O marvelous old man,
The methods of your art to scan,
'Yet here no instruments there be
Nor 'ometer nor 'scope I see.
'Did you (if questions you permit)
At the asylum leave your kit?'
That strange old man with motion rude
Grew to surprising altitude.
'Tools (and sarcazzems too) I scorns
I tells the weather by my corns.
'No doors and windows here you see
The wind and m'isture enters free.
'No fires nor lights, no wool nor fur
Here falsifies the tempercher.
'My corns unleathered I expose
To feel the rain's foretellin' throes.
'No stockin' from their ears keeps out
The comin' tempest's warnin' shout.

'Sich delicacy some has got
They know next summer's to be hot.
'This here one says (for that he's best):
'Storm center passin' to the west.'
'This feller's vitals is transfixed
With frost for Janawary sixt'.
'One chap jes' now is occy'pied
In fig'rin on next Fridy's tide.
'I've shaved this cuss so thin and true
He'll spot a fog in South Peru.
'Sech are my tools, which ne'er a swell
Observatory can excel.
'By long a-studyin' their throbs
I catches onto all the probs.'
Much more, no doubt, he would have said,
But suddenly he turned and fled;
For in mine eye's indignant green
Lay storms that he had not foreseen,
Till all at once, with silent squeals,
His toes 'caught on' and told his heels.

The Wise And Good
'O father, I saw at the church as I passed
The populace gathered in numbers so vast
That they couldn't get in; and their voices were low,
And they looked as if suffering terrible woe.'
''Twas the funeral, child, of a gentleman dead
For whom the great heart of humanity bled.'
'What made it bleed, father, for every day
Somebody passes forever away?
Do the newspaper men print a column or more
Of every person whose troubles are o'er?'
'O, no; they could never do that - and indeed,
Though printers might print it, no reader would read.
To the sepulcher all, soon or late, must be borne,
But 'tis only the Wise and the Good that all mourn.'
'That's right, father dear, but how can our eyes
Distinguish in dead men the Good and the Wise?'
'That's easy enough to the stupidest mind:
They're poor, and in dying leave nothing behind.'
'Seest thou in mine eye, father, anything green?
And takest thy son for a gaping marine?
Go tell thy fine tale of the Wise and the Good
Who are poor and lamented to babes in the wood.'
And that horrible youth as I hastened away
Was building a wink that affronted the day.

The Woful Tale Of Mr. Peters

I should like, good friends, to mention the disaster which befell
Mr. William Perry Peters, of the town of Muscatel,
Whose fate is full of meaning, if correctly understood
Admonition to the haughty, consolation to the good.
It happened in the hot snap which we recently incurred,
When 'twas warm enough to carbonize the feathers of a bird,
And men exclaimed: 'By Hunky!' who were bad enough to swear,
And pious persons supervised their adjectives with care.
Mr. Peters was a pedagogue of honor and repute,
His learning comprehensive, multifarious, minute.
It was commonly conceded in the section whence he came
That the man who played against him needed knowledge of the game.
And some there were who whispered, in the town of Muscatel,
That besides the game of Draw he knew Orthography as well;
Though, the school directors, frigidly contemning that as stuff,
Thought that Draw (and maybe Spelling, if it pleased him) was enough.
Withal, he was a haughty man - indubitably great,
But too vain of his attainments and his power in debate.
His mien was contumelious to men of lesser gift:
'It's only me,' he said, 'can give the human mind a lift.
'Before a proper audience, if ever I've a chance,
You'll see me chipping in, the cause of Learning to advance.
Just let me have a decent chance to back my mental hand
And I'll come to center lightly in a way they'll understand.'
Such was William Perry Peters, and I feel a poignant sense
Of grief that I'm unable to employ the present tense;
But Providence disposes, be our scheming what it may,
And disposed of Mr. Peters in a cold, regardless way.
It occurred in San Francisco, whither Mr. Peters came
In the cause of Education, feeling still the holy flame
Of ambition to assist in lifting up the human mind
To a higher plane of knowledge than its Architect designed.
He attended the convention of the pedagogic host;
He was first in the Pavilion, he was last to leave his post.
For days and days he narrowly observed the Chairman's eye,
His efforts ineffectual to catch it on the fly.
The blessed moment came at last: the Chairman tipped his head.
'The gentleman from ah - um - er,' that functionary said.
The gentleman from ah - um - er reflected with a grin:
'They'll know me better by - and - by, when I'm a-chipping in.'
So William Perry Peters mounted cheerfully his feet
And straightway was aglow with an incalculable heat!
His face was as effulgent as a human face could be,
And caloric emanated from his whole periphery;
For he felt himself the focus of non-Muscatelish eyes,
And the pain of their convergence was a terror and surprise.
As with pitiless impaction all their heat-waves on him broke
He was seen to be evolving awful quantities of smoke!
'Put him out!' cried all in chorus; but the meaning wasn't clear
Of that succoring suggestion to his obfuscated ear;

And it notably augmented his incinerating glow
To regard himself excessive, or in any way de trop.
Gone was all his wild ambition to lift up the human mind!
Gone the words he would have uttered! - gone the thought that lay behind!
For 'words that burn' may be consumed in a superior flame,
And 'thoughts that breathe' may breathe their last, and die a death of shame.
He'd known himself a shining light, but never had he known
Himself so very luminous as now he knew he shone.
'A pillar, I, of fire,' he'd said, 'to guide my race will be;'
And now that very inconvenient thing to him was he.
He stood there all irresolute; the seconds went and came;
The minutes passed and did but add fresh fuel to his flame.
How long he stood he knew not - 'twas a century or more
And then that incandescent man levanted for the door!
He darted like a comet from the building to the street,
Where Fahrenheit attested ninety-five degrees of heat.
Vicissitudes of climate make the tenure of the breath
Precarious, and William Perry Peters froze to death!

The Woman And The Devil

When Man and Woman had been made,
All but the disposition,
The Devil to the workshop strayed,
And somehow gained admission.
The Master rested from his work,
For this was on a Sunday,
The man was snoring like a Turk,
Content to wait till Monday.
'Too bad!' the Woman cried; 'Oh, why,
Does slumber not benumb me?
A disposition! Oh, I die
To know if 'twill become me!'
The Adversary said: 'No doubt
'Twill be extremely fine, ma'am,
Though sure 'tis long to be without
I beg to lend you mine, ma'am.'
The Devil's disposition when
She'd got, of course she wore it,
For she'd no disposition then,
Nor now has, to restore it.

The Yearly Lie

A merry Christmas? Prudent, as I live!
You wish me something that you need not give.
Merry or sad, what does it signify?
To you 't is equal if I laugh, or die.
Your hollow greeting, like a parrot's jest,

Finds all its meaning in the ear addressed.
Why 'merry' Christmas? Faith, I'd rather frown
Than grin and caper like a tickled clown.
When fools are merry the judicious weep;
The wise are happy only when asleep.
A present? Pray you give it to disarm
A man more powerful to do you harm.
'T was not your motive? Well, I cannot let
You pay for favors that you'll never get.
Perish the savage custom of the gift,
Founded in terror and maintained in thrift!
What men of honor need to aid their weal
They purchase, or, occasion serving, steal.
Go celebrate the day with turkeys, pies,
Sermons and psalms, and, for the children, lies.
Let Santa Claus descend again the flue;
If Baby doubt it, swear that it is true.
'A lie well stuck to is as good as truth,'
And God's too old to legislate for youth.
Hail Christmas! On my knees and fowl I fall:
For greater grace and better gravy call.
Vive l'Humbug! - that's to say, God bless us all!

Thersites

So, in the Sunday papers you, Del Mar,
Damn, all great Englishmen in English speech?
I am no Englishman, but in my reach
A rogue shall never rail where heroes are.
You are the man, if I mistake you not,
Who lately with a supplicating twitch
Plucked at the pockets of the London rich
And paid your share-engraver all you got.
Because that you have greatly lied, because
You libel nations, and because no hand
Of officer is raised to bid you stand,
And falsehood is unpunished of the laws,
I stand here in a public place to mark
With level finger where you part the crowd
I stand to name you and to cry aloud:
'Behold mendacity's great hierarch!'

Three Kinds Of A Rogue

Sharon, ambitious of immortal shame,
Fame's dead-wall daubed with his illustrious name
Served in the Senate, for our sins, his time,
Each word a folly and each vote a crime;
Law for our governance well skilled to make

By knowledge gained in study how to break;
Yet still by the presiding eye ignored,
Which only sought him when too loud he snored.
Auspicious thunder! - when he woke to vote
He stilled his own to cut his country's throat;
That rite performed, fell off again to sleep,
While statesmen ages dead awoke to weep!
For sedentary service all unfit,
By lying long disqualified to sit,
Wasting below as he decayed aloft,
His seat grown harder as his brain grew soft,
He left the hall he could not bring away,
And grateful millions blessed the happy day!
Whate'er contention in that hall is heard,
His sovereign State has still the final word:
For disputatious statesmen when they roar
Startle the ancient echoes of his snore,
Which from their dusty nooks expostulate
And close with stormy clamor the debate.
To low melodious thunders then they fade;
Their murmuring lullabies all ears invade;
Peace takes the Chair; the portal Silence keeps;
No motion stirs the dark Lethean deeps
Washoe has spoken and the Senate sleeps.
Lo! the new Sharon with a new intent,
Making no laws, but keen to circumvent
The laws of Nature (since he can't repeal)
That break his failing body on the wheel.
As Tantalus again and yet again
The elusive wave endeavors to restrain
To slake his awful thirst, so Sharon tries
To purchase happiness that age denies;
Obtains the shadow, but the substance goes,
And hugs the thorn, but cannot keep the rose;
For Dead Sea fruits bids prodigally, eats,
And then, with tardy reformation cheats.
Alert his faculties as three score years
And four score vices will permit, he nears
Dicing with Death - the finish of the game,
And curses still his candle's wasting flame,
The narrow circle of whose feeble glow
Dims and diminishes at every throw.
Moments his losses, pleasures are his gains,
Which even in his grasp revert to pains.
The joy of grasping them alone remains.
Ring up the curtain and the play protract!
Behold our Sharon in his last mad act.
With man long warring, quarreling with God,
He crouches now beneath a woman's rod
Predestined for his back while yet it lay
Closed in an acorn which, one luckless day,

He stole, unconscious of its foetal twig,
From the scant garner of a sightless pig.
With bleeding shoulders pitilessly scored,
He bawls more lustily than once he snored.
The sympathetic Comstocks droop to hear,
And Carson river sheds a viscous tear,
Which sturdy tumble-bugs assail amain,
With ready thrift, and urge along the plain.
The jackass rabbit sorrows as he lopes;
The sage-brush glooms along the mountain slopes;
In rising clouds the poignant alkali,
Tearless itself, makes everybody cry.
Washoe canaries on the Geiger Grade
Subdue the singing of their cavalcade,
And, wiping with their ears the tears unshed,
Grieve for their family's unlucky head.
Virginia City intermits her trade
And well-clad strangers walk her streets unflayed.
Nay, all Nevada ceases work to weep
And the recording angel goes to sleep.
But in his dreams his goose-quill's creaking fount
Augments the debits in the long account.
And still the continents and oceans ring
With royal torments of the Silver King!
Incessant bellowings fill all the earth,
Mingled with inextinguishable mirth.
He roars, men laugh, Nevadans weep, beasts howl,
Plash the affrighted fish, and shriek the fowl!
With monstrous din their blended thunders rise,
Peal upon peal, and brawl along the skies,
Startle in hell the Sharons as they groan,
And shake the splendors of the great white throne!
Still roaring outward through the vast profound,
The spreading circles of receding sound
Pursue each other in a failing race
To the cold confines of eternal space;
There break and die along that awful shore
Which God's own eyes have never dared explore
Dark, fearful, formless, nameless evermore!
Look to the west! Against yon steely sky
Lone Mountain rears its holy cross on high.
About its base the meek-faced dead are laid
To share the benediction of its shade.
With crossed white hands, shut eyes and formal feet,
Their nights are innocent, their days discreet.
Sharon, some years, perchance, remain of life
Of vice and greed, vulgarity and strife;
And then - God speed the day if such His will
You'll lie among the dead you helped to kill,
And be in good society at last,
Your purse unsilvered and your face unbrassed.

Tidings Of Good

Old Nick from his place of last resort
Came up and looked the world over.
He saw how the grass of the good was short
And the wicked lived in clover.
And he gravely said: 'This is all, all wrong,
And never by me intended.
If to me the power should ever belong
I shall have this thing amended.'
He looked so solemn and good and wise
As he made this observation
That the men who heard him believed their eyes
Instead of his reputation.
So they bruited the matter about, and each
Reported the words as nearly
As memory served - with additional speech
To bring out the meaning clearly.
The consequence was that none understood,
And the wildest rumors started
Of something intended to help the good
And injure the evil-hearted.
Then Robert Morrow was seen to smile
With a bright and lively joyance.
'A man,' said he, 'that is free from guile
Will now be free from annoyance.
'The Featherstones doubtless will now increase
And multiply like the rabbits,
While jailers, deputy sheriffs, police,
And writers will form good habits.
'The widows more easily robbed will be,
And no juror will ever heed 'em,
But open his purse to my eloquent plea
For security, gain, or freedom.'
When Benson heard of the luck of the good
(He was eating his dinner) he muttered:
'It cannot help me, for 'tis understood
My bread is already buttered.
'My plats of surveys are all false, they say,
But that cannot greatly matter
To me, for I'll tell the jurors that they
May lick, if they please, my platter.'

Tinker Dick

Good Parson Dickson preached, I'm told,
A sermon - ah, 'twas very old
And very, very, bald!
'Twas all about - I know not what

It was about, nor what 'twas not.
'A Screw Loose' it was called.
Whatever, Parson Dick, you say,
The world will get each blessed day
Still more and more askew,
And fall apart at last. Great snakes!
What skillful tinker ever takes
His tongue to turn a screw?

To A Censor

Delay responsible? Why, then; my friend,
Impeach Delay and you will make an end.
Thrust vile Delay in jail and let it rot
For doing all the things that it should not.
Put not good-natured judges under bond,
But make Delay in damages respond.
Minos, Aeacus, Rhadamanthus, rolled
Into one pitiless, unsmiling scold
Unsparing censor, be your thongs uncurled
To 'lash the rascals naked through the world.'
The rascals? Nay, Rascality's the thing
Above whose back your knotted scourges sing.
Your satire, truly, like a razor keen,
'Wounds with a touch that's neither felt nor seen;'
For naught that you assail with falchion free
Has either nerves to feel or eyes to see.
Against abstractions evermore you charge
You hack no helmet and you need no targe.
That wickedness is wrong and sin a vice,
That wrong's not right and foulness never nice,
Fearless affirm. All consequences dare:
Smite the offense and the offender spare.
When Ananias and Sapphira lied
Falsehood, had you been there, had surely died.
When money-changers in the Temple sat,
At money-changing you'd have whirled the 'cat'
(That John-the-Baptist of the modern pen)
And all the brokers would have cried amen!
Good friend, if any judge deserve your blame
Have you no courage, or has he no name?
Upon his method will you wreak your wrath,
Himself all unmolested in his path?
Fall to! fall to! - your club no longer draw
To beat the air or flail a man of straw.
Scorn to do justice like the Saxon thrall
Who cuffed the offender's shadow on a wall.
Let rascals in the flesh attest your zeal
Knocked on the mazzard or tripped up at heel!
We know that judges are corrupt. We know

That crimes are lively and that laws are slow.
We know that lawyers lie and doctors slay;
That priests and preachers are but birds of pray;
That merchants cheat and journalists for gold
Flatter the vicious while at vice they scold.
'Tis all familiar as the simple lore
That two policemen and two thieves make four.
But since, while some are wicked, some are good,
(As trees may differ though they all are wood)
Names, here and there, to show whose head is hit,
The bad would sentence and the good acquit.
In sparing everybody none you spare:
Rebukes most personal are least unfair.
To fire at random if you still prefer,
And swear at Dog but never kick a cur,
Permit me yet one ultimate appeal
To something that you understand and feel:
Let thrift and vanity your heart persuade
You might be read if you would learn your trade.
Good brother cynics (you have doubtless guessed
Not one of you but all are here addressed)
Remember this: the shaft that seeks a heart
Draws all eyes after it; an idle dart
Shot at some shadow flutters o'er the green,
Its flight unheeded and its fall unseen.

To A Critic Of Tennyson
Affronting fool, subdue your transient light;
When Wisdom's dull dares Folly to be bright:
If Genius stumble in the path to fame,
'Tis decency in dunces to go lame.

To A Dejected Poet
Thy gift, if that it be of God,
Thou hast no warrant to appraise,
Nor say: 'Here part, O Muse, our ways,
The road too stony to be trod.'
Not thine to call the labor hard
And the reward inadequate.
Who haggles o'er his hire with Fate
Is better bargainer than bard.
What! count the effort labor lost
When thy good angel holds the reed?
It were a sorry thing indeed
To stay him till thy palm be crossed.
'The laborer is worthy' - nay,
The sacred ministry of song

Is rapture! - 't were a grievous wrong
To fix a wages - rate for play.

To A Professional Eulogist
Newman, in you two parasites combine:
As tapeworm and as graveworm too you shine.
When on the virtues of the quick you've dwelt,
The pride of residence was all you felt
(What vain vulgarian the wish ne'er knew
To paint his lodging a flamboyant hue?)
And when the praises of the dead you've sung,
'Twas appetite, not truth, inspired your tongue;
As ill-bred men when warming to their wine
Boast of its merit though it be but brine.
Nor gratitude incites your song, nor should
Even charity would shun you if she could.
You share, 'tis true, the rich man's daily dole,
But what you get you take by way of toll.
Vain to resist you - vermifuge alone
Has power to push you from your robber throne.
When to escape you he's compelled to die
Hey! presto! - in the twinkling of an eye
You vanish as a tapeworm, reappear
As graveworm and resume your curst career.
As host no more, to satisfy your need
He serves as dinner your unaltered greed.
O thrifty sycophant of wealth and fame,
Son of servility and priest of shame,
While naught your mad ambition can abate
To lick the spittle of the rich and great;
While still like smoke your eulogies arise
To soot your heroes and inflame our eyes;
While still with holy oil, like that which ran
Down Aaron's beard, you smear each famous man,
I cannot choose but think it very odd
It ne'er occurs to you to fawn on God.

To A Stray Dog
Well, Towser (I'm thinking your name must be Towser),
You're a decentish puppy as puppy dogs go,
For you never, I'm sure, could have dined upon trowser,
And your tail's unimpeachably curled just so.
But, dear me! your name - if 'tis yours - is a 'poser':
Its meaning I cannot get anywise at,
When spoken correctly perhaps it is Toser,
And means one who toses. Max Muller, how's that?
I ne'er was ingenious at all at divining

A word's prehistorical, primitive state,
Or finding its root, like a mole, by consigning
Its bloom to the turnep-top's sorrowful fate.
And, now that I think of it well, I'm no nearer
The riddle's solution than ever - for how's
My pretty invented word, 'tose,' any clearer
In point of its signification than 'towse'?
So, Towser (or Toser), I mean to rename you
In honor of some good and eminent man,
In the light and the heat of whose quickening fame you
May grow to an eminent dog if you can.
In sunshine like his you'll not long be a croucher:
The Senate shall hear you - for that I will vouch.
Come here, sir. Stand up. I rechristen you Goucher.
But damn you! I'll shoot you if ever you gouch!

To A Summer Poet
Yes, the Summer girl is flirting on the beach,
With a him.
And the damboy is a-climbing for the peach,
On the limb;
Yes, the bullfrog is a-croaking
And the dudelet is a-smoking
Cigarettes;
And the hackman is a-hacking
And the showman is a-cracking
Up his pets;
Yes, the Jersey 'skeeter flits along the shore
And the snapdog - we have heard it o'er and o'er;
Yes, my poet,
Well we know it
Know the spooners how they spoon
In the bright
Dollar light
Of the country tavern moon;
Yes, the caterpillars fall
From the trees (we know it all),
And with beetles all the shelves
Are alive.
Please unbuttonhole us - O,
Have the grace to let us go,
For we know
How you Summer poets thrive,
By the recapitulation
And insistent iteration
Of the wondrous doings incident to Life
Among Ourselves!
So, I pray you stop the fervor and the fuss.
For you, poor human linnet,

There's a half a living in it,
But there's not a copper cent in it for us!

To A Word-Warrior
Frank Pixley, you, who kiss the hand
That strove to cut the country's throat,
Cannot forgive the hands that smote
Applauding in a distant land,
Applauding carelessly, as one
The weaker willing to befriend
Until the quarrel's at an end,
Then learn by whom it was begun.
When North was pitted against South
Non-combatants on either side
In calculating fury vied,
And fought their foes by word of mouth.
That devil's-camisade you led
With formidable feats of tongue.
Upon the battle's rear you hung
With Samson's weapon slew the dead!
So hot the ardor of your soul
That every fierce civilian came,
His torch to kindle at your name,
Or have you blow his cooling coal.
Men prematurely left their beds
And sought the gelid bath - so great
The heat and splendor of your hate
Of Englishmen and 'Copperheads.'
King Liar of deceitful men,
For imposition doubly armed!
The patriots whom your speaking charmed
You stung to madness with your pen.
There was a certain journal here,
Its English owner growing rich
Your hand the treason wrote for which
A mob cut short its curst career.
If, Pixley, you had not the brain
To know the true from false, or you
To Truth had courage to be true,
And loyal to her perfect reign;
If you had not your powers arrayed
To serve the wrong by tricksy speech,
Nor pushed yourself within the reach
Of retribution's accolade,
I had not had the will to go
Outside the olive-bordered path
Of peace to cut the birch of wrath,
And strip your body for the blow.
Behold how dark the war-clouds rise

About the mother of our race!
The lightnings gild her tranquil face
And glitter in her patient eyes.
Her children throng the hither flood
And lean intent above the beach.
Their beating hearts inhibit speech
With stifling tides of English blood.
'Their skies, but not their hearts, they change
Who go in ships across the sea'
Through all centuries to be
The strange new land will still be strange.
The Island Mother holds in gage
The souls of sons she never saw;
Superior to law, the law
Of sympathetic heritage.
Forgotten now the foolish reign
Of wrath which sundered trivial ties.
A soldier's sabre vainly tries
To cleave a spiritual chain.
The iron in our blood affines,
Though fratricidal hands may spill.
Shall Hate be throned on Bunker Hill,
Yet Love abide at Seven Pines?

To An Aspirant
What! you a Senator - you, Mike de Young?
Still reeking of the gutter whence you sprung?
Sir, if all Senators were such as you,
Their hands so crimson and so slender, too,
(Shaped to the pocket for commercial work,
For literary, fitted to the dirk)
So black their hearts, so lily-white their livers,
The toga's touch would give a man the shivers.

To An Insolent Attorney
So, Hall McAllister, you'll not be warned
My protest slighted, admonition scorned!
To save your scoundrel client from a cell
As loth to swallow him as he to swell
Its sum of meals insurgent (it decries
All wars intestinal with meats that rise)
You turn your scurril tongue against the press
And damn the agency you ought to bless.
Had not the press with all its hundred eyes
Discerned the wolf beneath the sheep's disguise
And raised the cry upon him, he to-day
Would lack your company, and you would lack his pay.

Talk not of 'hire' and consciences for sale
You whose profession 'tis to threaten, rail,
Calumniate and libel at the will
Of any villain who can pay the bill
You whose most honest dollars all were got
By saying for a fee 'the thing that's not!'
To you 'tis one, to challenge or defend;
Clients are means, their money is an end.
In my profession sometimes, as in yours
Always, a payment large enough secures
A mercenary service to defend
The guilty or the innocent to rend.
But mark the difference, nor think it slight:
We do not hold it proper, just and right;
Of selfish lies a little still we shame
And give our villainies another name.
Hypocrisy's an ugly vice, no doubt,
But blushing sinners can't get on without.
Happy the lawyer! - at his favored hands
Nor truth nor decency the world demands.
Secure in his immunity from shame,
His cheek ne'er kindles with the tell-tale flame.
His brains for sale, morality for hire,
In every land and century a licensed liar!
No doubt, McAllister, you can explain
How honorable 'tis to lie for gain,
Provided only that the jury's made
To understand that lying is your trade.
A hundred thousand volumes, broad and flat,
(The Bible not included) proving that,
Have been put forth, though still the doubt remains
If God has read them with befitting pains.
No Morrow could get justice, you'll declare,
If none who knew him foul affirmed him fair.
Ingenious man! how easy 'tis to raise
An argument to justify the course that pays!
I grant you, if you like, that men may need
The services performed for crime by greed,
Grant that the perfect welfare of the State
Requires the aid of those who in debate
As mercenaries lost in early youth
The fine distinction between lie and truth
Who cheat in argument and set a snare
To take the feet of Justice unaware
Who serve with livelier zeal when rogues assist
With perjury, embracery (the list
Is long to quote) than when an honest soul,
Scorning to plot, conspire, intrigue, cajole,
Reminds them (their astonishment how great!)
He'd rather suffer wrong than perpetrate.
I grant, in short, 'tis better all around

That ambidextrous consciences abound
In courts of law to do the dirty work
That self-respecting scavengers would shirk.
What then? Who serves however clean a plan
By doing dirty work, he is a dirty man!

To 'Colonel' Dan. Burns
They say, my lord, that you're a Warwick. Well,
The title's an absurd one, I believe:
You make no kings, you have no kings to sell,
Though really 'twere easy to conceive
You stuffing half-a-dozen up your sleeve.
No, you're no Warwick, skillful from the shell
To hatch out sovereigns. On a mare's nest, maybe,
You'd incubate a little jackass baby.
I fancy, too, that it is naught but stuff,
This 'power' that you're said to be 'behind
The throne.' I'm sure 'twere accurate enough
To represent you simply as inclined
To push poor Markham (ailing in his mind
And body, which were never very tough)
Round in an invalid's wheeled chair. Such menial
Employment to low natures is congenial.
No, Dan, you're an impostor every way:
A human bubble, for 'the earth,' you know,
'Hath bubbles, as the water hath.' Some day
Some careless hand will prick your film, and O,
How utterly you'll vanish! Daniel, throw
(As fallen Woolsey might to Cromwell say)
Your curst ambition to the pigs - though truly
'Twould make them greater pigs, and more unruly.

To E.S. Salomon
What! Salomon! such words from you,
Who call yourself a soldier? Well,
The Southern brother where he fell
Slept all your base oration through.
Alike to him - he cannot know
Your praise or blame: as little harm
Your tongue can do him as your arm
A quarter-century ago.
The brave respect the brave. The brave
Respect the dead; but you - you draw
That ancient blade, the ass's jaw,
And shake it o'er a hero's grave.
Are you not he who makes to-day
A merchandise of old renown

Which he persuades this easy town
He won in battle far away?
Nay, those the fallen who revile
Have ne'er before the living stood
And stoutly made their battle good
And greeted danger with a smile.
What if the dead whom still you hate
Were wrong? Are you so surely right?
We know the issue of the fight
The sword is but an advocate.
Men live and die, and other men
Arise with knowledges diverse:
What seemed a blessing seems a curse,
And Now is still at odds with Then.
The years go on, the old comes back
To mock the new - beneath the sun.
Is nothing new; ideas run
Recurrent in an endless track.
What most we censure, men as wise
Have reverently practiced; nor
Will future wisdom fail to war
On principles we dearly prize.
We do not know - we can but deem,
And he is loyalest and best
Who takes the light full on his breast
And follows it throughout the dream.
The broken light, the shadows wide
Behold the battle-field displayed!
God save the vanquished from the blade,
The victor from the victor's pride!
If, Salomon, the blessed dew
That falls upon the Blue and Gray
Is powerless to wash away
The sin of differing from you.
Remember how the flood of years
Has rolled across the erring slain;
Remember, too, the cleansing rain
Of widows' and of orphans' tears.
The dead are dead - let that atone:
And though with equal hand we strew
The blooms on saint and sinner too,
Yet God will know to choose his own.
The wretch, whate'er his life and lot,
Who does not love the harmless dead
With all his heart and all his head
May God forgive him - I shall not.
When, Salomon, you come to quaff
The Darker Cup with meeker face,
I, loving you at last, shall trace
Upon your tomb this epitaph:
'Draw near, ye generous and brave

Kneel round this monument and weep:
It covers one who tried to keep
A flower from a dead man's grave.'

To E.S. Salomon

What! Salomon! such words from you,
Who call yourself a soldier? Well,
The Southern brother where he fell
Slept all your base oration through.
Alike to him - he cannot know
Your praise or blame: as little harm
Your tongue can do him as your arm
A quarter-century ago.
The brave respect the brave. The brave
Respect the dead; but you - you draw
That ancient blade, the ass's jaw,
And shake it o'er a hero's grave.
Are you not he who makes to-day
A merchandise of old reknown
Which he persuades this easy town
He won in battle far away?
Nay, those the fallen who revile
Have ne'er before the living stood
And stoutly made their battle good
And greeted danger with a smile.
What if the dead whom still you hate
Were wrong? Are you so surely right?
We know the issues of the fight
The sword is but an advocate.
Men live and die, and other men
Arise with knowledges diverse:
What seemed a blessing seems a curse,
And Now is still at odds with Then.
The years go on, the old comes back
To mock the new - beneath the sun
Is nothing new; ideas run
Recurrent in an endless track.
What most we censure, men as wise
Have reverently practiced; nor
Will future wisdom fail to war
On principles we dearly prize.
We do not know - we can but deem,
And he is loyalest and best
Who takes the light full on his breast
And follows it throughout the dream.
The broken light, the shadows wide
Behold the battle-field displayed!
God save the vanquished from the blade,
The victor from the victor's pride.

If, Salomon, the blessed dew
That falls upon the Blue and Gray
Is powerless to wash away
The sin of differing from you,
Remember how the flood of years
Has rolled across the erring slain;
Remember, too, the cleansing rain
Of widows' and of orphans' tears.
The dead are dead - let that atone:
And though with equal hand we strew
The blooms on saint and sinner too,
Yet God will know to choose his own.
The wretch, whate'er his life and lot,
Who does not love the harmless dead
With all his heart and all his head
May God forgive him, I shall not.
When, Salomon, you come to quaff
The Darker Cup with meeker face,
I, loving you at last, shall trace
Upon your tomb this epitaph:
'Draw near, ye generous and brave
Kneel round this monument and weep
For one who tried in vain to keep
A flower from a soldier's grave.'

To Either
Back further than
I know, in San
Francisco dwelt a wealthy man.
So rich was he
That none could be
Wise, good and great in like degree.
'Tis true he wrought,
In deed or thought,
But few of all the things he ought;
But men said: 'Who
Would wish him to?
Great souls are born to be, not do!'
One thing, indeed,
He did, we read,
Which was becoming, all agreed:
Grown provident,
Ere life was spent
He built a mighty monument.
For longer than
I know, in San
Francisco lived a beggar man;
And when in bed
They found him dead

'Just like the scamp!' the people said.
He died, they say,
On the same day
His wealthy neighbor passed away.
What matters it
When beggars quit
Their beats? I answer: Not a bit.
They got a spade
And pick and made
A hole, and there the chap was laid.
'He asked for bread,'
'Twas neatly said:
'He'll get not even a stone instead.'
The years rolled round:
His humble mound
Sank to the level of the ground;
And men forgot
That the bare spot
Was like (and was) the beggar's lot.
Forgotten, too,
Was t'other, who
Had reared the monument to woo
Inconstant Fame,
Though still his name
Shouted in granite just the same.
That name, I swear,
They both did bear
The beggar and the millionaire.
That lofty tomb,
Then, honored - whom?
For argument here's ample room.
I'll not debate,
But only state
The scamp first claimed it at the Gate.
St. Peter, proud
To serve him, bowed
And showed him to the softest cloud.

To Her
O, Sinner A, to me unknown
Be such a conscience as your own!
To ease it you to Sinner B
Confess the sins of Sinner C.

To Maude
Not as two errant spheres together grind
With monstrous ruin in the vast of space,

Destruction born of that malign embrace,
Their hapless peoples all to death consigned
Not so when our intangible worlds of mind,
Even mine and yours, each with its spirit race
Of beings shadowy in form and face,
Shall drift together on some blessed wind.
No, in that marriage of gloom and light
All miracles of beauty shall be wrought,
Attesting a diviner faith than man's;
For all my sad-eyed daughters of the night
Shall smile on your sweet seraphim of thought,
Nor any jealous god forbid the banns.

To My Laundress
Saponacea, wert thou not so fair
I'd curse thee for thy multitude of sins
For sending home my clothes all full of pins
A shirt occasionally that's a snare
And a delusion, got, the Lord knows where,
The Lord knows why-a sock whose outs and ins
None know, nor where it ends nor where begins,
And fewer cuffs than ought to be my share.
But when I mark thy lilies how they grow,
And the red roses of thy ripening charms,
I bless the lovelight in thy dark eyes dreaming.
I'll never pay thee, but I'd gladly go
Into the magic circle of thine arms,
Supple and fragrant from repeated steaming.

To My Liars
Attend, mine enemies of all degrees,
From sandlot orators and sandlot fleas
To fallen gentlemen and rising louts
Who babble slander at your drinking bouts,
And, filled with unfamiliar wine, begin
Lies drowned, ere born, in more congenial gin.
But most attend, ye persons of the press
Who live (though why, yourselves alone can guess)
In hope deferred, ambitious still to shine
By hating me at half a cent a line
Like drones among the bees of brighter wing,
Sunless to shine and impotent to sting.
To estimate in easy verse I'll try
The controversial value of a lie.
So lend your ears - God knows you have enough!
I mean to teach, and if I can't I'll cuff.
A lie is wicked, so the priests declare;

But that to us is neither here nor there.
'Tis worse than wicked, it is vulgar too;
N'importe - with that we've nothing here to do.
If 'twere artistic I would lie till death,
And shape a falsehood with my latest breath.
Parrhasius never more did pity lack,
The while his model writhed upon the rack,
Than I for my collaborator's pain,
Who, stabbed with fibs again and yet again,
Would vainly seek to move my stubborn heart
If slander were, and wit were not, an art.
The ill-bred and illiterate can lie
As fast as you, and faster far than I.
Shall I compete, then, in a strife accurst
Where Allen Forman is an easy first,
And where the second prize is rightly flung
To Charley Shortridge or to Mike de Young?
In mental combat but a single end
Inspires the formidable to contend.
Not by the raw recruit's ambition fired,
By whom foul blows, though harmless, are admired;
Not by the coward's zeal, who, on his knee
Behind the bole of his protecting tree,
So curves his musket that the bark it fits,
And, firing, blows the weapon into bits;
But with the noble aim of one whose heart
Values his foeman for he loves his art
The veteran debater moves afield,
Untaught to libel as untaught to yield.
Dear foeman mine, I've but this end in view
That to prevent which most you wish to do.
What, then, are you most eager to be at?
To hate me? Nay, I'll help you, sir, at that.
This only passion does your soul inspire:
You wish to scorn me. Well, you shall admire.
'Tis not enough my neighbors that you school
In the belief that I'm a rogue or fool;
That small advantage you would gladly trade
For what one moment would yourself persuade.
Write, then, your largest and your longest lie:
You sha'n't believe it, howsoe'er you try.
No falsehood you can tell, no evil do,
Shall turn me from the truth to injure you.
So all your war is barren of effect;
I find my victory in your respect.
What profit have you if the world you set
Against me? For the world will soon forget
It thought me this or that; but I'll retain
A vivid picture of your moral stain,
And cherish till my memory expire
The sweet, soft consciousness that you're a liar

Is it your triumph, then, to prove that you
Will do the thing that I would scorn to do?
God grant that I forever be exempt
From such advantage as my foe's contempt.

To Nanine

Dear, if I never saw your face again;
If all the music of your voice were mute
As that of a forlorn and broken lute;
If only in my dreams I might attain
The benediction of your touch, how vain
Were Faith to justify the old pursuit
Of happiness, or Reason to confute
The pessimist philosophy of pain.
Yet Love not altogether is unwise,
For still the wind would murmur in the corn,
And still the sun would splendor all the mere;
And I - I could not, dearest, choose but hear
Your voice upon the breeze and see your eyes
Shine in the glory of the summer morn.

To One Across The Way

When at your window radiant you've stood
I've sometimes thought - forgive me if I've erred
That some slight thought of me perhaps has stirred
Your heart to beat less gently than it should.
I know you beautiful; that you are good
I hope - or fear - I cannot choose the word,
Nor rightly suit it to the thought. I've heard
Reason at love's dictation never could.
Blindly to this dilemma so I grope,
As one whose every pathway has a snare:
If you are minded in the saintly fashion
Of your pure face my passion's without hope;
If not, alas! I equally despair,
For what to me were hope without the passion?

To One Detested

Sir, you're a veteran, revealed
In history and fable
As warrior since you took the field,
Defeating Abel.
As Commissary later (or
If not, in every cottage
The tale is) you contracted for

A mess of pottage.
In civil life you were, we read
(And our respect increases)
A man of peace - a man, indeed,
Of thirty pieces.
To paying taxes when you turned
Your mind, or what you call so,
A wide celebrity you earned
Saphira also.
In every age, by various names,
You've won renown in story,
But on your present record flames
A greater glory.
Cain, Esau, and Iscariot, too,
And Ananias, likewise,
Each had peculiar powers, but who
Could lie as Mike lies?

To Oscar Wilde
Because from Folly's lips you got
Some babbled mandate to subdue
The realm of Common Sense, and you
Made promise and considered not
Because you strike a random blow
At what you do not understand,
And beckon with a friendly hand
To something that you do not know,
I hold no speech of your desert,
Nor answer with porrected shield
The wooden weapon that you wield,
But meet you with a cast of dirt.
Dispute with such a thing as you
Twin show to the two-headed calf?
Why, sir, if I repress my laugh,
'T is more than half the world can do.

To The Bartholdi Statue
O Liberty, God-gifted
Young and immortal maid
In your high hand uplifted;
The torch declares your trade.
Its crimson menace, flaming
Upon the sea and shore,
Is, trumpet-like, proclaiming
That Law shall be no more.
Austere incendiary,
We're blinking in the light;

Where is your customary
Grenade of dynamite?
Where are your staves and switches
For men of gentle birth?
Your mask and dirk for riches?
Your chains for wit and worth?
Perhaps, you've brought the halters
You used in the old days,
When round religion's altars
You stabled Cromwell's bays?
Behind you, unsuspected,
Have you the axe, fair wench,
Wherewith you once collected
A poll-tax from the French?
America salutes you
Preparing to disgorge.
Take everything that suits you,
And marry Henry George.

To The Fool-Killer
Ah, welcome, welcome! Sit you down, old friend;
Your pipe I'll serve, your bottle I'll attend.
'Tis many a year since you and I have known
Society more pleasant than our own
In our brief respites from excessive work
I pointing out the hearts for you to dirk.
What have you done since lately at this board
We canvassed the deserts of all the horde
And chose what names would please the people best,
Engraved on coffin-plates - what bounding breast
Would give more satisfaction if at rest?
But never mind - the record cannot fail:
The loftiest monuments will tell the tale.
I trust ere next we meet you'll slay the chap
Who calls old Tyler 'Judge' and Merry 'Cap'
Calls John P. Irish 'Colonel' and John P.,
Whose surname Jack-son speaks his pedigree,
By the same title - men of equal rank
Though one is belly all, and one all shank,
Showing their several service in the fray:
One fought for food and one to get away.
I hope, I say, you'll kill the 'title' man
Who saddles one on every back he can,
Then rides it from Beersheba to Dan!
Another fool, I trust, you will perform
Your office on while my resentment's warm:
He shakes my hand a dozen times a day
If, luckless, I so often cross his way,
Though I've three senses besides that of touch,

To make me conscious of a fool too much.
Seek him, friend Killer, and your purpose make
Apparent as his guilty hand you take,
And set him trembling with a solemn: 'Shake!'
But chief of all the addle-witted crew
Conceded by the Hangman's League to you,
The fool (his dam's acquainted with a knave)
Whose fluent pen, of his no-brain the slave,
Strews notes of introduction o'er the land
And calls it hospitality - his hand
May palsy seize ere he again consign
To me his friend, as I to Hades mine!
Pity the wretch, his faults howe'er you see,
Whom A accredits to his victim, B.
Like shuttlecock which battledores attack
(One speeds it forward, one would drive it back)
The trustful simpleton is twice unblest
A rare good riddance, an unwelcome guest.
The glad consignor rubs his hands to think
How duty is commuted into ink;
The consignee (his hands he cannot rub
He has the man upon them) mutters: 'Cub!'
And straightway plans to lose him at the Club.
You know, good Killer, where this dunce abides
The secret jungle where he writes and hides
Though no exploring foot has e'er upstirred
His human elephant's exhaustless herd.
Go, bring his blood! We'll drink it - letting fall
A due libation to the gods of Gall.
On second thought, the gods may have it all.

To The Happy Hunting Grounds
Wide windy reaches of high stubble field;
A long gray road, bordered with dusty pines;
A wagon moving in a 'cloud by day.'
Two city sportsmen with a dove between,
Breast-high upon a fence and fast asleep
A solitary dove, the only dove
In twenty counties, and it sick, or else
It were not there. Two guns that fire as one,
With thunder simultaneous and loud;
Two shattered human wrecks of blood and bone!
And later, in the gloaming, comes a man
The worthy local coroner is he,
Renowned all thereabout, and popular
With many a remain. All tenderly
Compiling in a game-bag the debris,
He glides into the gloom and fades from sight.
The dove, cured of its ailment by the shock,

Has flown, meantime, on pinions strong and fleet,
To die of age in some far foreign land.

To-Day
I saw a man who knelt in prayer,
And heard him say:
'I'll lay my inmost spirit bare
To-day.
'Lord, for to-morrow and its need
I do not pray;
Let me upon my neighbor feed
To-day.
'Let me my duty duly shirk
And run away
From any form or phase of work
To-day.
'From Thy commands exempted still
Let me obey
The promptings of my private will
To-day.
'Let me no word profane, no lie
Unthinking say
If anyone is standing by
To-day.
'My secret sins and vices grave
Let none betray;
The scoffer's jeers I do not crave
To-day.
'And if to-day my fortune all
Should ebb away,
Help me on other men's to fall
To-day.
'So, for to-morrow and its mite
I do not pray;
Just give me everything in sight
To-day.'
I cried: 'Amen!' He rose and ran
Like oil away.
I said: 'I've seen an honest man
To-day.'

Twin Unworthies
Ye parasites that to the rich men stick,
As to the fattest sheep the thrifty tick
Ed'ard to Stanford and to Crocker Ben
(To Ben and Ed'ard many meaner men,
And lice to these) who do the kind of work

That thieves would have the honesty to shirk
Whose wages are that your employers own
The fat that reeks upon your every bone
And deigns to ask (the flattery how sweet!)
About its health and how it stands the heat,
Hail and farewell! I meant to write about you,
But, no, my page is cleaner far without you.

Two Methods
To bucks and ewes by the Good Shepherd fed
The Priest delivers masses for the dead,
And even from estrays outside the fold
Death for the masses he would not withhold.
The Parson, loth alike to free or kill,
Forsakes the souls already on the grill,
And, God's prerogative of mercy shamming,
Spares living sinners for a harder damning.

Two Rogues
Dim, grim, and silent as a ghost,
The sentry occupied his post,
To all the stirrings of the night
Alert of ear and sharp of sight.
A sudden something - sight or sound,
About, above, or underground,
He knew not what, nor where - ensued,
Thrilling the sleeping solitude.
The soldier cried: 'Halt! Who goes there?'
The answer came: 'Death - in the air.'
'Advance, Death - give the countersign,
Or perish if you cross that line!'
To change his tone Death thought it wise
Reminded him they 'd been allies
Against the Russ, the Frank, the Turk,
In many a bloody bit of work.
'In short,' said he, 'in every weather
We've soldiered, you and I, together.'
The sentry would not let him pass.
'Go back,' he growled, 'you tiresome ass
Go back and rest till the next war,
Nor kill by methods all abhor:
Miasma, famine, filth and vice,
With plagues of locusts, plagues of lice,
Foul food, foul water, and foul gases,
Rank exhalations from morasses.
If you employ such low allies
This business you will vulgarize.

Renouncing then the field of fame
To wallow in a waste of shame,
I'll prostitute my strength and lurk
About the country doing work
These hands to labor I'll devote,
Nor cut, by Heaven, another throat!'

Two Shows
The showman (blessing in a thousand shapes!)
Parades a 'School of Educated Apes!'
Small education's needed, I opine,
Or native wit, to make a monkey shine;
The brute exhibited has naught to do
But ape the larger apes who come to view
The hoodlum with his horrible grimace,
Long upper lip and furtive, shuffling pace,
Significant reminders of the time
When hunters, not policemen, made him climb;
The lady loafer with her draggling 'trail,'
That free translation of an ancient tail;
The sand-lot quadrumane in hairy suit,
Whose heels are thumbs perverted by the boot;
The painted actress throwing down the gage
To elder artists of the sylvan stage,
Proving that in the time of Noah's flood
Two ape-skins held her whole profession's blood;
The critic waiting, like a hungry pup,
To write the school - perhaps to eat it up,
As chance or luck occasion may reveal
To earn a dollar or maraud a meal.
To view the school of apes these creatures go,
Unconscious that themselves are half the show.
These, if the simian his course but trim
To copy them as they have copied him,
Will call him 'educated.' Of a verity
There's much to learn by study of posterity.

Two Statesmen
In that fair city by the inland sea,
Where Blaine unhived his Presidential bee,
Frank Pixley's meeting with George Gorham sing,
Celestial muse, and what events did spring
From the encounter of those mighty sons
Of thunder, and of slaughter, and of guns.
Great Gorham first, his yearning tooth to sate
And give him stomach for the day's debate,
Entering a restaurant, with eager mien,

Demands an ounce of bacon and a bean.
The trembling waiter, by the statesman's eye
Smitten with terror, hastens to comply;
Nor chairs nor tables can his speed retard,
For famine's fixed and horrible regard
He takes for menace. As he shaking flew,
Lo! the portentous Pixley heaved in view!
Before him yawned invisible the cell,
Unheard, behind, the warden's footsteps fell.
Thrice in convention rising to his feet,
He thrice had been thrust back into his seat;
Thrice had protested, been reminded thrice
The nation had no need of his advice.
Balked of his will to set the people right,
His soul was gloomy though his hat was white,
So fierce his mien, with provident accord
The waiters swarmed him, thinking him a lord.
He spurned them, roaring grandly to their chief:
'Give me (Fred. Crocker pays) a leg of beef!'
His wandering eye's deluminating flame
Fell upon Gorham and the crisis came!
For Pixley scowled and darkness filled the room
Till Gorham's flashing orbs dispelled the gloom.
The patrons of the place, by fear dismayed,
Sprang to the street and left their scores unpaid.
So, when Jove thunders and his lightnings gleam
To sour the milk and curdle, too, the cream,
And storm-clouds gather on the shadowed hill,
The ass forsakes his hay, the pig his swill.
Hotly the heroes now engaged their breath
Came short and hard, as in the throes of death.
They clenched their hands, their weapons brandished high,
Cut, stabbed, and hewed, nor uttered any cry,
But gnashed their teeth and struggled on! In brief,
One ate his bacon, t'other one his beef.

Unarmed

Saint Peter sat at the jasper gate,
When Stephen M. White arrived in state.
'Admit me.' 'With pleasure,' Peter said,
Pleased to observe that the man was dead;
'That's what I'm here for. Kindly show
Your ticket, my lord, and in you go.'
White stared in blank surprise. Said he
'I run this place - just turn that key.'
'Yes?' said the Saint; and Stephen heard
With pain the inflection of that word.
But, mastering his emotion, he
Remarked: 'My friend, you're too d-- free;

'I'm Stephen M., by thunder, White!'
And, 'Yes?' the guardian said, with quite
The self-same irritating stress
Distinguishing his former yes.
And still demurely as a mouse
He twirled the key to that Upper House.
Then Stephen, seeing his bluster vain
Admittance to those halls to gain,
Said, neighborly: 'Pray tell me. Pete,
Does any one contest my seat?'
The Saint replied: 'Nay, nay, not so;
But you voted always wrong below:
'Whate'er the question, clear and high
You're voice rang: 'I,' 'I,' ever 'I.''
Now indignation fired the heart
Of that insulted immortal part.
'Die, wretch!' he cried, with blanching lip,
And made a motion to his hip,
With purpose murderous and hearty,
To draw the Democratic party!
He felt his fingers vainly slide
Upon his unappareled hide
(The dead arise from their 'silent tents'
But not their late habiliments)
Then wailed - the briefest of his speeches:
'I've left it in my other breeches!'

Uncoloneled

Though war-signs fail in time of peace, they say,
Two awful portents gloom the public mind:
All Mexico is arming for the fray
And Colonel Mark McDonald has resigned!
We know not by what instinct he divined
The coming trouble may be, like the steed
Described by Job, he smelled the fight afar.
Howe'er it be, he left, and for that deed
Is an aspirant to the G.A.R.
When cannon flame along the Rio Grande
A citizen's commission will be handy.

Unexpounded

On Evidence, on Deeds, on Bills,
On Copyhold, on Loans, on Wills,
Lawyers great books indite;
The creaking of their busy quills
I've never heard on Right.

Vanished At Cock-Crow

'I've found the secret of your charm,' I said,
Expounding with complacency my guess.
Alas! the charm, even as I named it, fled,
For all its secret was unconsciousness.

Vice Versa

Down in the state of Maine, the story goes,
A woman, to secure a lapsing pension,
Married a soldier - though the good Lord knows
That very common act scarce calls for mention.
What makes it worthy to be writ and read
The man she married had been nine hours dead!
Now, marrying a corpse is not an act
Familiar to our daily observation,
And so I crave her pardon if the fact
Suggests this interesting speculation:
Should some mischance restore the man to life
Would she be then a widow, or a wife?
Let casuists contest the point; I'm not
Disposed to grapple with so great a matter.
'T would tie my thinker in a double knot
And drive me staring mad as any hatter
Though I submit that hatters are, in fact,
Sane, and all other human beings cracked.
Small thought have I of Destiny or Chance;
Luck seems to me the same thing as Intention;
In metaphysics I could ne'er advance,
And think it of the Devil's own invention.
Enough of joy to know though when I wed
I must be married, yet I may be dead.

Visions Of Sin

KRASLAJORSK, SIBERIA, March 29.
'My eyes are better, and I shall travel slowly toward home.'
DANENHOWER.

From the regions of the Night,
Coming with recovered sight
From the spell of darkness free,
What will Danenhower see?
He will see when he arrives,
Doctors taking human lives.
He will see a learned judge
Whose decision will not budge

Till both litigants are fleeced
And his palm is duly greased.
Lawyers he will see who fight
Day by day and night by night;
Never both upon a side,
Though their fees they still divide.
Preachers he will see who teach
That it is divine to preach
That they fan a sacred fire
And are worthy of their hire.
He will see a trusted wife
(Pride of some good husband's life)
Enter at a certain door
And - but he will see no more.
He will see Good Templars reel
See a prosecutor steal,
And a father beat his child.
He'll perhaps see Oscar Wilde.
From the regions of the Night
Coming with recovered sight
From the bliss of blindness free,
That's what Danenhower'll see.

Weather

Once I dipt into the future far as human eye could see,
And I saw the Chief Forecaster, dead as any one can be
Dead and damned and shut in Hades as a liar from his birth,
With a record of unreason seldome paralleled on earth.
While I looked he reared him solemnly, that incandescent youth,
From the coals that he'd preferred to the advantages of truth.
He cast his eyes about him and above him; then he wrote
On a slab of thin asbestos what I venture here to quote
For I read it in the rose-light of the everlasting glow:
'Cloudy; variable winds, with local showers; cooler; snow.'

With a Book

Words shouting, singing, smiling, frowning
Sense lacking.
Ah, nothing, more obscure than Browning,
Save blacking.

With Mine Own Petard

Time was the local poets sang their songs
Beneath their breath in terror of the thongs
I snapped about their shins. Though mild the stroke

Bards, like the conies, are 'a feeble folk,'
Fearing all noises but the one they make
Themselves - at which all other mortals quake.
Now from their cracked and disobedient throats,
Like rats from sewers scampering, their notes
Pour forth to move, where'er the season serves,
If not our legs to dance, at least our nerves;
As once a ram's-horn solo maddened all
The sober-minded stones in Jerich's wall.
A year's exemption from the critic's curse
Mends the bard's courage but impairs his verse.
Thus poolside frogs, when croaking in the night,
Are frayed to silence by a meteor's flight,
Or by the sudden plashing of a stone
From some adjacent cottage garden thrown,
But straight renew the song with double din
Whene'er the light goes out or man goes in.
Shall I with arms unbraced (my casque unlatched,
My falchion pawned, my buckler, too, attached)
Resume the cuishes and the broad cuirass,
Accomplishing my body all in brass,
And arm in battle royal to oppose
A village poet singing through the nose,
Or strolling troubadour his lyre who strums
With clumsy hand whose fingers all are thumbs?
No, let them rhyme; I fought them once before
And stilled their songs - but, Satan! how they swore!
Cuffed them upon the mouth whene'er their throats
They cleared for action with their sweetest notes;
Twisted their ears (they'd oft tormented mine)
And damned them roundly all along the line;
Clubbed the whole crew from the Parnassian slopes,
A wreck of broken heads and broken hopes!
What gained I so? I feathered every curse
Launched at the village bards with lilting verse.
The town approved and christened me (to show its
High admiration) Chief of Local Poets!

Woman In Politics

What, madam, run for School Director? You?
And want my vote and influence? Well, well,
That beats me! Gad! where are we drifting to?
In all my life I never have heard tell
Of such sublime presumption, and I smell
A nigger in the fence! Excuse me, madam;
We statesmen sometimes speak like the old Adam.
But now you mention it - well, well, who knows?
We might, that's certain, give the sex a show.
I have a cousin - teacher. I suppose

If I stand in and you 're elected - no?
You'll make no bargains? That's a pretty go!
But understand that school administration
Belongs to Politics, not Education.
We'll pass the teacher deal; but it were wise
To understand each other at the start.
You know my business - books and school supplies;
You'd hardly, if elected, have the heart
Some small advantage to deny me - part
Of all my profits to be yours. What? Stealing?
Please don't express yourself with so much feeling.
You pain me, truly. Now one question more.
Suppose a fair young man should ask a place
As teacher - would you (pardon) shut the door
Of the Department in his handsome face
Until I know not how to put the case
Would you extort a kiss to pay your favor?
Good Lord! you laugh? I thought the matter graver.
Well, well, we can't do business, I suspect:
A woman has no head for useful tricks.
My profitable offers you reject
And will not promise anything to fix
The opposition. That's not politics.
Good morning. Stay - I'm chaffing you, conceitedly.
Madam, I mean to vote for you - repeatedly.

Y'e Foe To Cathaye

O never an oathe sweares he,
And never a pig-taile jerkes;
With a brick-batte he ne lurkes
For to buste y'e crust, perdie,
Of y'e man from over sea,
A-synging as he werkes.
For he knows ful well, y's youth,
A tricke of exceeding worth:
And he plans withouten ruth
A conflagration's birth!

Ye Idyll Of Ye Hippopopotamus

With a Methodist hymn in his musical throat,
The Sun was emitting his ultimate note;
His quivering larynx enwrinkled the sea
Like an Ichthyosaurian blowing his tea;
When sweetly and pensively rattled and rang
This plaint which an Hippopopotamus sang:
'O, Camomile, Calabash, Cartilage-pie,
Spread for my spirit a peppermint fry;

Crown me with doughnuts, and drape me with cheese,
Settle my soul with a codliver sneeze.
Lo, how I stand on my head and repine
Lollipop Lumpkin can never be mine!'
Down sank the Sun with a kick and a plunge,
Up from the wave rose the head of a Sponge;
Ropes in his ringlets, eggs in his eyes,
Tip-tilted nose in a way to surprise.
These the conundrums he flung to the breeze,
The answers that Echo returned to him these:
'Cobblestone, Cobblestone, why do you sigh
Why do you turn on the tears?'
'My mother is crazy on strawberry jam,
And my father has petrified ears.'
'Liverwort, Liverwort, why do you droop
Why do you snuffle and scowl?'
'My brother has cockle-burs into his eyes,
And my sister has married an owl.'
'Simia, Simia, why do you laugh
Why do you cackle and quake?'
'My son has a pollywog stuck in his throat,
And my daughter has bitten a snake.'
Slow sank the head of the Sponge out of sight,
Soaken with sea-water - then it was night.
The Moon had now risen for dinner to dress,
When sweetly the Pachyderm sang from his nest;
He sang through a pestle of silvery shape,
Encrusted with custard - empurpled with crape;
And this was the burden he bore on his lips,
And blew to the listening Sturgeon that sips
From the fountain of opium under the lobes
Of the mountain whose summit in buffalo robes
The winter envelops, as Venus adorns
An elephant's trunk with a chaplet of thorns:
'Chasing mastodons through marshes upon stilts of light ratan,
Hunting spiders with a shotgun and mosquitoes with an axe,
Plucking peanuts ready roasted from the branches of the oak,
Waking echoes in the forest with our hymns of blessed bosh,
We roamed - my love and I.
By the margin of the fountain spouting thick with clabbered milk,
Under spreading boughs of bass-wood all alive with cooing toads,
Loafing listlessly on bowlders of octagonal design,
Standing gracefully inverted with our toes together knit,
We loved - my love and I.'
Hippopopotamus comforts his heart
Biting half-moons out of strawberry tart.
Epitaph on George Francis Train.
(Inscribed on a Pork-barrel.)
Beneath this casket rots unknown
A Thing that merits not a stone,
Save that by passing urchin cast;

Whose fame and virtues we express
By transient urn of emptiness,
With apt inscription (to its past
Relating - and to his): 'Prime Mess.'
No honour had this infidel,
That doth not appertain, as well,
To altered caitiff on the drop;
No wit that would not likewise pass
For wisdom in the famished ass
Who breaks his neck a weed to crop,
When tethered in the luscious grass.
And now, thank God, his hateful name
Shall never rescued be from shame,
Though seas of venal ink be shed;
No sophistry shall reconcile
With sympathy for Erin's Isle,
Or sorrow for her patriot dead,
The weeping of this crocodile.
Life's incongruity is past,
And dirt to dirt is seen at last,
The worm of worm afoul doth fall.
The sexton tolls his solemn bell
For scoundrel dead and gone to-well,
It matters not, it can't recall
This convict from his final cell.
Jerusalem, Old and New.
Didymus Dunkleton Doty Don John
Is a parson of high degree;
He holds forth of Sundays to marvelling crowds
Who wonder how vice can still be
When smitten so stoutly by Didymus Don
Disciple of Calvin is he.
But sinners still laugh at his talk of the
New Jerusalem - ha - ha, te - he!
And biting their thumbs at the doughty
Don-John This parson of high degree
They think of the streets of a village they know,
Where horses still sink to the knee,
Contrasting its muck with the pavement of gold
That's laid in the other citee.
They think of the sign that still swings, uneffaced
By winds from the salt, salt sea,
Which tells where he trafficked in tipple, of yore
Don Dunkleton Johnny, D. D.
Didymus Dunkleton Doty Don John
Still plays on his fiddle-D. D.,
His lambkins still bleat in full psalmody sweet,
And the devil still pitches the key.
Communing with Nature.
One evening I sat on a heavenward hill,
The winds were asleep and all nature was still,

Wee children came round me to play at my knee,
As my mind floated rudderless over the sea.
I put out one hand to caress them, but held
With the other my nose, for these cherubim smelled.
I cast a few glances upon the old sun;
He was red in the face from the race he had run,
But he seemed to be doing, for aught I could see,
Quite well without any assistance from me.
And so I directed my wandering eye
Around to the opposite side of the sky,
And the rapture that ever with ecstasy thrills
Through the heart as the moon rises bright from the hills,
Would in this case have been most exceedingly rare,
Except for the fact that the moon was not there.
But the stars looked right lovingly down in the sea,
And, by Jupiter, Venus was winking at me!
The gas in the city was flaring up bright,
Montgomery Street was resplendent with light;
But I did not exactly appear to advance
A sentiment proper to that circumstance.
So it only remains to explain to the town
That a rainstorm came up before I could come down.
As the boots I had on were uncommonly thin
My fancy leaked out as the water leaked in.
Though dampened my ardour, though slackened my strain,
I'll 'strike the wild lyre' who sings the sweet rain!
Conservatism and Progress.
Old Zephyr, dawdling in the West,
Looked down upon the sea,
Which slept unfretted at his feet,
And balanced on its breast a fleet
That seemed almost to be
Suspended in the middle air,
As if a magnet held it there,
Eternally at rest.
Then, one by one, the ships released
Their folded sails, and strove
Against the empty calm to press
North, South, or West, or East,
In vain; the subtle nothingness
Was impotent to move.
Ten Zephyr laughed aloud to see:
'No vessel moves except by me,
And, heigh-ho! I shall sleep.'
But lo! from out the troubled North
A tempest strode impatient forth,
And trampled white the deep;
The sloping ships flew glad away,
Laving their heated sides in spray.
The West then turned him red with wrath,
And to the North he shouted:

'Hold there! How dare you cross my path,
As now you are about it?'
The North replied with laboured breath
His speed no moment slowing:
'My friend, you'll never have a path,
Unless you take to blowing.'
Inter Arma Silent Leges.
(An Election Incident.)
About the polls the freedmen drew,
To vote the freemen down;
And merrily their caps up-flew
As Grant rode through the town.
From votes to staves they next did turn,
And beat the freemen down;
Full bravely did their valour burn
As Grant rode through the town.
Then staves for muskets they forsook,
And shot the freemen down;
Right royally their banners shook
As Grant rode through the town.
Hail, final triumph of our cause!
Hail, chief of mute renown!
Grim Magistrate of Silent Laws,
A-riding freedom down!

Quintessence
'To produce these spicy paragraphs, which have been unsuccessfully imitated by every newspaper in the State, requires the combined efforts of five able-bodied persons associated on the editorial staff of this journal.' - New York Herald.

Sir Muscle speaks, and nations bend the ear:
'Hark ye these Notes - our wit quintuple hear;
Five able-bodied editors combine
Their strength prodigious in each laboured line!'
O wondrous vintner! hopeless seemed the task
To bung these drainings in a single cask;
The riddle's read-five leathern skins contain
The working juice, and scarcely feel the strain.
Saviours of Rome! will wonders never cease?
A ballad cackled by five tuneful geese!
Upon one Rosinante five stout knights
Ride fiercely into visionary fights!
A cap and bells five sturdy fools adorn,
Five porkers battle for a grain of corn,
Five donkeys squeeze into a narrow stall,
Five tumble-bugs propel a single ball!
Resurgam.
Dawns dread and red the fateful morn
Lo, Resurrection's Day is born!

The striding sea no longer strides,
No longer knows the trick of tides;
The land is breathless, winds relent,
All nature waits the dread event.
From wassail rising rather late,
Awarding Jove arrives in state;
O'er yawning graves looks many a league,
Then yawns himself from sheer fatigue.
Lifting its finger to the sky,
A marble shaft arrests his eye
This epitaph, in pompous pride,
Engraven on its polished side:
'Perfection of Creation's plan,
Here resteth Universal Man,
Who virtues, segregated wide,
Collated, classed, and codified,
Reduced to practice, taught, explained,
And strict morality maintained.
Anticipating death, his pelf
He lavished on this monolith;
Because he leaves nor kin nor kith
He rears this tribute to himself,
That Virtue's fame may never cease.
His jacet - let him rest in peace!'
With sober eye Jove scanned the shaft,
Then turned away and lightly laughed
'Poor Man! since I have careless been
In keeping books to note thy sin,
And thou hast left upon the earth
This faithful record of thy worth,
Thy final prayer shall now be heard:
Of life I'll not renew thy lease,
But take thee at thy carven word,
And let thee rest in solemn peace!'

Yorick
Hard by an excavated street one sat
In solitary session on the sand;
And ever and anon he spake and spat
And spake again - a yellow skull in hand,
To which that retrospective Pioneer
Addressed the few remarks that follow here:
'Who are you? Did you come 'der blains agross,'
Or 'Horn aroundt'? In days o' '49
Did them thar eye-holes see the Southern
Cross From the Antarctic Sea git up an' shine?
Or did you drive a bull team 'all the way
From Pike,' with Mr. Joseph Bowers? - say!
'Was you in Frisco when the water came

Up to Montgum'ry street? and do you mind
The time when Peters run the faro game
Jim Peters from old Mississip - behind
Wells Fargo's, where he subsequent was bust
By Sandy, as regards both bank and crust?
'I wonder was you here when Casey shot
James King o' William? And did you attend
The neck-tie dance ensuin'? I did not,
But j'ined the rush to Go Creek with my friend
Ed'ard McGowan; for we was resolved
In sech diversions not to be involved.
'Maybe I knowed you; seems to me I've seed
Your face afore. I don't forget a face,
But names I disremember - I'm that breed
Of owls. I'm talking some'at into space
An' maybe my remarks is too derned free,
Seein' yer name is unbeknown to me.
'Ther' was a time, I reckon, when I knowed
Nigh onto every dern galoot in town.
That was as late as '50. Now she's growed
Surprisin'! Yes, me an' my pardner, Brown,
Was wide acquainted. If ther' was a cuss
We didn't know, the cause was - he knowed us.
'Maybe you had that claim adjoinin' mine
Up thar in Calaveras. Was it you
To which Long Mary took a mighty shine,
An' throwed squar' off on Jake the Kangaroo?
I guess if she could see ye now she'd take
Her chance o' happiness along o' Jake.
'You ain't so purty now as you was then:
Yer eyes is nothin' but two prospect holes,
An' women which are hitched to better men
Would hardly for sech glances damn their souls,
As Lengthie did. By G--! I hope it's you,
For' (kicks the skull) 'I'm Jake the Kangaroo.'

Aspirants Three

DRAMATIS PERSONAE.
QUICK:
DE YOUNG a Brother to Mushrooms
DEAD:
SWIFT an Heirloom
ESTEE a Relic
IMMORTALS:
THE SPIRIT OF BROKEN HOPES. THE AUTHOR.
MISCELLANEOUS:
A TROUPE OF COFFINS. THE MOON. VARIOUS COLORED FIRES.

Scene - The Political Graveyard at Bone Mountain.

DE YOUNG:
This is the spot agreed upon. Here rest
The sainted statesman who upon the field
Of honor have at various times laid down
Their own, and ended, ignominious,
Their lives political. About me, lo!
Their silent headstones, gilded by the moon,
Half-full and near her setting-midnight. Hark!
Through the white mists of this portentous night
(Which throng in moving shapes about my way,
As they were ghosts of candidates I've slain,
To fray their murderer) my open ear,
Spacious to maw the noises of the world,
Engulfs a footstep.

(Enter Estee from his tomb.)

Ah, 'tis he, my foe,
True to appointment; and so here we fight
Though truly 'twas my firm belief that he
Would send regrets, or I had not been here.

ESTEE:
O moon that hast so oft surprised the deeds
Whereby I rose to greatness! - tricksy orb,
The type and symbol of my politics,
Now draw my ebbing fortunes to their flood,
As, by the magic of a poultice, boils
That burn ambitions with defeated fires
Are lifted into eminence.

(Sees De Young.)

What? you!
Faith, if I had suspected you would come
From the fair world of politics wherein
So lately you were whelped, and which, alas,
I vainly to revisit strive, though still
Rapped on the rotting head and bidden sleep
Till Resurrection's morn, if I had thought
You would accept the challenge that I flung
I would have seen you damned ere
I came forth In the night air, shroud-clad and shivering,
To fight so mean a thing! But since you're here,
Draw and defend yourself. By gad, we'll see
Who'll be Postmaster-General!

DE YOUNG:

We will
I'll fight (for I am lame) with any blue
And redolent remain that dares aspire
To wreck the Grand Old Grandson's cabinet.
Here's at you, nosegay!

(They draw tongues and are about to fight, when from an adjacent whited sepulcher, enter Swift.)

SWIFT:
Hold! put up your tongues!
Within the confines of this sacred spot
Broods such a holy calm as none may break
By clash of weapons, without sacrilege.
(Beats down their tongues with a bone.)
Madmen! what profits it? For though you fought
With such heroic skill that both survived,
Yet neither should achieve the prize, for I
Would wrest it from him. Let us not contend,
But friendliwise by stipulation fix
A slate for mutual advantage. Why,
Having the pick and choice of seats, should we
Forego them all but one? Nay, we'll take three,
And part them so among us that to each
Shall fall the fittest to his powers. In brief,
Let us establish a Portfolio Trust.

ESTEE:
Agreed.

DE YOUNG:
Aye, truly, 'tis a greed - and one
The offices imperfectly will sate,
But I'll stand in.

SWIFT:
Well, so 'tis understood,
As you're the junior member of the Trust,
Politically younger and undead,
Speak, Michael: what portfolio do you choose?

DE YOUNG:
I've thought the Postal service best would serve
My interest; but since I have my pick,
I'll take the War Department. It is known
Throughout the world, from Market street to Pine,
(For a Chicago journal told the tale)
How in this hand I lately took my life
And marched against great Buckley, thundering
My mandate that he count the ballots fair!
Earth heard and shrank to half her size! Yon moon,
Which rivaled then a liver's whiteness, paused

That night at Butchertown and daubed her face
With sheep's blood! Then my serried rank I drew
Back to my stronghold without loss. To mark
My care in saving human life and limb,
The Peace Society bestowed on me
Its leather medal and the title, too,
Of Colonel. Yes, my genius is for war. Good land!
I naturally dote on a brass band!

(Sings.)
O, give me a life on the tented field,
Where the cannon roar and ring,
Where the flag floats free and the foemen yield
And bleed as the bullets sing.
But be it not mine to wage the fray
Where matters are ordered the other way,
For that is a different thing.
O, give me a life in the fierce campaign
Let it be the life of my foe:
I'd rather fall upon him than the plain;
That service I'd fain forego.
O, a warrior's life is fine and free,
But a warrior's death - ah me! ah me!
That's a different thing, you know.

ESTEE:
Some claim I might myself advance to that
Portfolio. When Rebellion raised its head,
And you, my friends, stayed meekly in your shirts,
I marched with banners to the party stump,

Spat on my hands, made faces fierce as death,
Shook my two fists at once and introduced
Brave resolutions terrible to read!
Nay, only recently, as you do know,
I conquered Treason by the word of mouth,
And slew, with Samson's weapon, the whole South!

SWIFT:
You once fought Stanford, too.

ESTEE:
Enough of that
Give me the Interior and I'll devote
My mind to agriculture and improve
The breed of cabbages, especially
The Brassica Celeritatis, named
For you because in days of long ago
You sold it at your market stall, and, faith,
'Tis said you were an honest huckster then.
I'll be Attorney-General if you

Prefer; for know I am a lawyer too!

SWIFT:
I never have heard that! did you, De Young?

DE YOUNG:
Never, so help me! And I swear I've heard
A score of Judges say that he is not.

SWIFT (to Estee):
You take the Interior. I might aspire
To military station too, for once
I led my party into Pixley's camp,
And he paroled me. I defended, too,
The State of Oregon against the sharp
And bloody tooth of the Australian sheep.
But I've an aptitude exceeding neat
For bloodless battles of diplomacy.
My cobweb treaty of Exclusion once,
Through which a hundred thousand coolies sailed,
Was much admired, but most by Colonel Bee.
Though born a tinker I'm a diplomat
From old Missouri, and I - ha! what's that?

(Exit Moon. Enter Blue Lights on all the tombs, and a circle of Red Fire on the grass; in the center the Spirit of Broken Hopes, and round about, a Troupe of Coffins, dancing and singing.)

CHORUS OF COFFINS:
Two bodies dead and one alive
Yo, ho, merrily all!
Now for boodle strain and strive
Buzzards all a-warble, O!
Prophets three, agape for bread;
Raven with a stone instead
Providential raven!
Judges two and Colonel one
Run, run, rustics, run!
But it's O, the pig is shaven,
And oily, oily all!
(Exeunt Coffins, dancing. The Spirit of Broken Hopes advances, solemnly pointing at each of the Three Worthies in turn.)

SPIRIT OF BROKEN HOPES:
Governor, Governor, editor man,
Rusty, musty, spick-and-span,
Harlequin, harridan, dicky-dout,
Demagogue, charlatan-o, u, t, OUT!
(De Young falls and sleeps.)
Antimonopoler, diplomat,
Railroad lackey, political rat,
One, two, three - SCAT!

(Swift falls and sleeps.)
Boycotting chin-worker, working to woo
Fortune, the fickle, to smile upon you,
Jo-coated acrobat, shuttle-cock-SHOO!

(Estee falls and sleeps.)

Now they lie in slumber sweet,
Now the charm is all complete,
Hasten I with flying feet
Where beyond the further sea
A babe upon its mother's knee
Is gazing into skies afar
And crying for a golden star.
I'll drag a cloud across the blue
And break that infant's heart in two!

(Exeunt the Spirit of Broken Hopes and the Red and Blue Fires. Re-enter Moon.) ESTEE (waking): Why, this is strange! I dreamed I know not what, It seemed that certain apparitions were,

Which sang uncanny words, significant
And yet ambiguous - half-understood
Portending evil; and an awful spook,
Even as I stood with my accomplices,
Counted me out, as children do in play.
Is that you, Mike?

DE YOUNG (waking):
It was.

SWIFT (waking):
Am I all that?
Then I'll reform my ways.

(Reforms his ways.)

Ah! had I known
How sweet it is to be an honest man
I never would have stooped to turn my coat
For public favor, as chameleons take
The hue (as near as they can judge) of that
Supporting them. Henceforth I'll buy
With money all the offices I need,
And know the pleasure of an honest life,
Or stay forever in this dismal place.
Now that I'm good, it will no longer do
To make a third with such, a wicked two.

(Returns to his tomb.)

DE YOUNG:

Prophetic dream! by some good angel sent
To make me with a quiet life content.
The question shall no more my bosom irk,
To go to Washington or go to work.
From Fame's debasing struggle I'll withdraw,
And taking up the pen lay down the law.
I'll leave this rogue, lest my example make
An honest man of him - his heart would break.

(Exit De Young.)

ESTEE:
Out of my company these converts flee,
But that advantage is denied to me:
My curst identity's confining skin
Nor lets me out nor tolerates me in.
Well, since my hopes eternally have fled,
And, dead before, I'm more than ever dead,
To find a grander tomb be now my task,
And pack my pork into a stolen cask.

(Exit, searching. Loud calls for the Author, who appears, bowing and smiling.)

AUTHOR (singing):
Jack Satan's the greatest of gods,
And Hell is the best of abodes.
'Tis reached, through the Valley of Clods,
By seventy different roads.
Hurrah for the Seventy Roads!
Hurrah for the clods that resound
With a hollow, thundering sound!
Hurrah for the Best of Abodes!
We'll serve him as long as we've breath
Jack Satan the greatest of gods.
To all of his enemies, death!
A home in the Valley of Clods.
Hurrah for the thunder of clods
That smother the soul of his foe!
Hurrah for the spirits that go
To dwell with the Greatest of Gods;
(Curtain falls to faint odor of mortality. Exit the Gas.)

Metempsychosis

DRAMATIS PERSONAE.
ST. JOHN a Presidential Candidate
MCDONALD a Defeated Aspirant
MRS. HAYES an Ex-President
PITTS-STEVENS a Water Nymph

Scene - A Small Lake in the Alleghany Mountains.

ST. JOHN:
Hours I've immersed my muzzle in this tarn
And, quaffing copious potations, tried
To suck it dry; but ever as I pumped
Its waters into my distended skin
The labor of my zeal extruded them
In perspiration from my pores; and so,
Rilling the marginal declivity,
They fell again into their source. Ah, me!
Could I but find within these ancient hills
Some long extinct volcano, by the rains
Of countless ages in its crater brimmed
Like a full goblet, I would lay me down
Prone on the outer slope, and o'er its edge
Arching my neck, I'd siphon out its store
And flood the valleys with my sweat for aye.
So should I be accounted as a god,
Even as Father Nilus is. What's that?
Methought I heard some sawyer draw his file
With jarring, stridulous cacophany
Across his notchy blade, to set its teeth
And mine on edge. Ha! there it goes again!
Song, within.
Cold water's the milk of the mountains,
And Nature's our wet-nurse. O then,
Glue thou thy blue lips to her fountains
Forever and ever, amen!

ST. JOHN:
Why surely there's congenial company
Aloof - the spirit, I suppose, that guards
This sacred spot; perchance some water-nymph
Who laving in the crystal flood her limbs
Has taken cold, and so, with raucous voice
Afflicts the sensitive membrane of mine ear
The while she sings my sentiments.

(Enter Pitts-Stevens.)

Hello!
What fiend is this?

PITTS-STEVENS:
'Tis I, be not afraid.

ST. JOHN:
And who, thou antiquated crone, art thou?
I ne'er forget a face, but names I can't

So well remember. I have seen thee oft.
When in the middle season of the night,
Curved with a cucumber, or knotted hard
With an eclectic pie, I've striven to keep
My head and heels asunder, thou has come,
With sociable familiarity,
Into my dream, but not, alas, to bless.

PITTS-STEVENS:
My name's Pitts-Stevens, age just seventeen years;
Talking teetotaler, professional
Beauty.

ST. JOHN:
What dost them here?

PITTS-STEVENS:
I'm come, fair sir,
With paint and brush to blazon on these rocks
The merits of my master's nostrum-so:

(Paints rapidly.)

'McDonald's Vinegar Bitters!'

ST. JOHN:
What are they?
PITTS-STEVENS:
A woman suffering from widowhood
Took a full bottle and was cured. A man
There was - a murderer; the doctors all
Had given him up - he'd but an hour to live.
He swallowed half a glassful. He is dead,
But not of Vinegar Bitters. A wee babe
Lay sick and cried for it. The mother gave
That innocent a spoonful and it smoothed
Its pathway to the tomb. 'Tis warranted
To cause a boy to strike his father, make
A pig squeal, start the hair upon a stone,
Or play the fiddle for a country dance.

(Enter McDonald, reading a Sunday-school book.)

Good morrow, sir; I trust you're well.

MCDONALD:
H'lo, Pitts!
Observe, good friends, I have a volume here
Myself am author of a noble book
To train the infant mind (delightful task!)
It tells how one Samantha Brown, age, six,

A gutter-bunking slave to rum, was saved
By Vinegar Bitters, went to church and now
Has an account at the Pacific Bank.
I'll read the whole work to you.

ST JOHN:
Heaven forbid!
I've elsewhere an engagement.

PITTS-STEVENS:
I am deaf.

MCDONALD (reading regardless):
'Once on a time there lived'

(Enter Mrs. Hayes.)

Behold our queen!

ALL:
Her eyes upon the ground
Before her feet she low'rs,
Walking, in thought profound,
As 'twere, upon all fours.
Her visage is austere,
Her gait a high parade;
At every step you hear
The sloshing lemonade!

MRS. HAYES (to herself):
Once, sitting in the White House, hard at work
Signing State papers (Rutherford was there,
Knitting some hose) a sudden glory fell
Upon my paper. I looked up and saw
An angel, holding in his hand a rod
Wherewith he struck me. Smarting with the blow
I rose and (cuffing Rutherford) inquired:
'Wherefore this chastisement?' The angel said:
'Four years you have been President, and still

There's rum!' - then flew to Heaven. Contrite, I swore
Such oath as lady Methodist might take,
My second term should medicine my first.
The people would not have it that way; so
I seek some candidate who'll take my soul
My spirit of reform, fresh from my breast,
And give me his instead; and thus equipped
With my imperious and fiery essence,
Drive the Drink Demon from the land and fill
The people up with water till their teeth
Are all afloat.

(St. John discovers himself.)

What, you?

ST. JOHN:
Aye, Madam, I'll
Swap souls with you and lead the cold sea-green
Amphibians of Prohibition on,
Pallid of nose and webbed of foot, swim-bladdered,
Gifted with gills, invincible!

MRS. HAYES:
Enough,
Stand forth and consummate the interchange.

(While McDonald and Pitts-Stevens modestly turn their backs, the latter blushing a delicate shrimp-pink, St. John and Mrs. Hayes effect an exchange of immortal parts. When the transfer is complete McDonald turns and advances, uncorking a bottle of Vinegar Bitters.)

MCDONALD (chanting):
Nectar compounded of simples
Cocted in Stygian shades
Acids of wrinkles and pimples
From faces of ancient maids
Acrid precipitates sunken
From tempers of scolding wives
Whose husbands, uncommonly drunken,
Are commonly found in dives,
With this I baptize and appoint thee
(to St. John.)
To marshal the vinophobe ranks.
In the name of Dambosh I anoint thee
(pours the liquid down St. John's back.)
As King of aquatical cranks!

(The liquid blisters the royal back, and His Majesty starts on a dead run, energetically exclaiming. Exit St. John.)

MRS. HAYES:
My soul! My soul! I'll never get it back
Unless I follow nimbly on his track.

(Exit Mrs. Hayes.)

PITTS-STEVENS:
O my! he's such a beautiful young man!
I'll follow, too, and catch him if I can.

(Exit Pitts-Stevens.)

MCDONALD:
He scarce is visible, his dust so great!
Methinks for so obscure a candidate
He runs quite well. But as for Prohibition
I mean myself to hold the first position.

(Produces a pocket flask, topes a cruel quantity of double-distilled thunder and lightning out of it, smiles so grimly as to darken all the stage and sings):

Though fortunes vary let all be merry,
And then if e'er a disaster befall,
At Styx's ferry is Charon's wherry
In easy call.
Upon a ripple of golden tipple
That tipsy ship'll convey you best.
To king and cripple, the bottle's the nipple
Of Nature's breast!

'Peaceable Expulsion'

DRAMATIS PERSONAE.
MOUNTWAVE a Politician
HARDHAND a Workingman
TOK BAK a Chinaman
SATAN a Friend to Mountwave
CHORUS OF FOREIGN VOTERS.

MOUNTWAVE:
My friend, I beg that you will lend your ears
(I know 'tis asking a good deal of you)
While I for your instruction nominate
Some certain wrongs you suffer. Men like you
Imperfectly are sensible of all
The miseries they actually feel.
Hence, Providence has prudently raised up
Clear-sighted men like me to diagnose
Their cases and inform them where they're hurt.
The wounds of honest workingmen I've made
A specialty, and probing them's my trade.

HARDHAND:
Well, Mister, s'pose you let yer bossest eye
Camp on my mortal part awhile; then you
Jes' toot my sufferin's an' tell me what's
The fashionable caper now in writhes
The very swellest wiggle.

MOUNTWAVE:
Well, my lad,

'Tis plain as is the long, conspicuous nose
Borne, ponderous and pendulous, between
The elephant's remarkable eye-teeth

(Enter Tok Bak.)

That Chinese competition's what ails you.

BOTH (Singing):
O pig-tail Celestial,
O barbarous bestial,
Abominable Chinee!
Simian fellow man,
Primitive yellow man,
Joshian devotee!
Shoe-and-cigar machine,
Oleomargarine
You are, and butter are we

Fat of the land are we,
Salt of the earth;
In God's image planned to be
Noble in birth!
You, on the contrary,
Modeled upon very
Different lines indeed,
Show in conspicuous,
Base and ridiculous
Ways your inferior breed.
Wretched apology,
Shame of ethnology,
Monster unspeakably low!
Fit to be buckshotted
Be you 'steboycotted.
Vanish-vamoose-mosy - Go!

TOK BAK:
You listen me! You beatee the big dlum
An' tell me go to Flowly Kingdom Come.
You all too muchee fool. You chinnee heap.
Such talkee like my washee-belly cheap!

(Enter Satan.)

You dlive me outee clunty towns all way;
Why you no tackle me Safflisco, hay?

SATAN:
Methought I heard a murmuring of tongues
Sound through the ceiling of the hollow earth,
As if the anti-coolie ques - ha! friends,

Well met. You see I keep my ancient word:
Where two or three are gathered in my name,
There am I in their midst.

MOUNTWAVE:
O monstrous thief!
To quote the words of Shakespeare as your own.
I know his work.

HARDHAND:
Who's Shakespeare? what's his trade?
I've heard about the work o' that galoot
Till I'm jest sick!

TOK BAK:
Go Sunny school - you'll know
Mo' Bible. Bime by pleach - hell - talkee. Tell
'Bout Abel - mebby so he live too cheap.
He mebby all time dig on lanch - no dlink,
No splee - no go plocession fo' make vote
No sendee money out of clunty fo'
To helpee Ilishmen. Cain killum. Josh
He catchee at it, an' he belly mad
Say: 'Allee Melicans boycottee Cain.'
Not muchee - you no pleachee that:
You all same lie.

MOUNTWAVE:
This cuss must be expelled.

(Draws pistol.)

MOUNTWAVE, HARDHAND, SATAN (singing):
For Chinese expulsion, hurrah!
To mobbing and murder, all hail!
Away with your justice and law
We'll make every pagan turn tail.

CHORUS OF FOREIGN VOTERS:
Bedad! oof dot tief o'ze vorld
Zat Ivan Tchanay vos got hurled
In Hella, da debil he say:
'Wor be yer return pairmit, hey?'
Und gry as 'e shaka da boot:
'Zis haythen haf nevaire been oot!'

HARDHAND:
Too many cooks are working at this broth
I think, by thunder, t'will be mostly froth!
I'm cussed ef I can sarvy, up to date,
What good this dern fandango does the State.

MOUNTWAVE:
The State's advantage, sir, you may not see,
But think how good it is for me.

SATAN:
And me.

(Curtain.)

Slander

FITCH:
'All vices you've exhausted, friend;
So all the papers say.'

PICKERING:
'Ah, what vile calumnies are penned!
'Tis just the other way.'

Slickens

DRAMATIS PERSONAE.
HAYSEED a Granger
NOZZLE a Miner
RINGDIVVY a Statesman
FEEGOBBLE a Lawyer
JUNKET a Committee

Scene - Yuba Dam.
Feegobble, Ringdivvy, Nozzle.

NOZZLE:
My friends, since '51 I have pursued
The evil tenor of my watery way,
Removing hills as by an act of faith

RINGDIVVY:
Just so; the steadfast faith of those who hold,
In foreign lands beyond the Eastern sea,
The shares in your concern - a simple, blind,
Unreasoning belief in dividends,
Still stimulated by assessments which,
When the skies fall, ensnaring all the larks,
Will bring, no doubt, a very great return.

ALL (singing):

O the beautiful assessment,
The exquisite assessment,
The regular assessment,
That makes the water flow.

RINGDIVVY:
The rascally assessment!

FEEGOBBLE:
The murderous assessment!

NOZZLE:
The glorious assessment
That makes my mare to go!

FEEGOBBLE:
But, Nozzle, you, I think, were on the point
Of making a remark about some rights
Some certain vested rights you have acquired
By long immunity; for still the law
Holds that if one do evil undisturbed
His right to do so ripens with the years;
And one may be a villain long enough
To make himself an honest gentleman.

ALL (singing):
Hail, holy law,
The soul with awe
Bows to thy dispensation.

NOZZLE:
It breaks my jaw!

RINGDIVVY:
It qualms my maw!

FEEGOBBLE:
It feeds my jaw,
It crams my maw,
It is my soul's salvation!

NOZZLE:
Why, yes, I've floated mountains to the sea
For lo! these many years; though some, they say,
Do strand themselves along the bottom lands
And cover up a village here and there,
And here and there a ranch. 'Tis said, indeed,
The granger with his female and his young
Do not infrequently go to the dickens
By premature burial in slickens.

ALL (singing):
Could slickens forever
Choke up the river,
And slime's endeavor
Be tried on grain,
How small the measure
Of granger's treasure,
How keen his pain!

RINGDIVVY:
'A consummation devoutly to be wished!'
These rascal grangers would long since have been
Submerged in slimes, to the last man of them,
But for the fact that all their wicked tribes
Affect our legislation with their bribes.

ALL (singing):
O bribery's great
'Tis a pillar of State,
And the people they are free.

FEEGOBBLE:
It smashes my slate!

NOZZLE:
It is thievery straight!

RINGDIVVY:
But it's been the making of me!

NOZZLE:
I judge by certain shrewd sensations here
In these callosities I call my thumbs
thrilling sense as of ten thousand pins,
Red-hot and penetrant, transpiercing all
The cuticle and tickling through the nerves
That some malign and awful thing draws near.

(Enter Hayseed.)

Good Lord! here are the ghosts and spooks of all
The grangers I have decently interred,
Rolled into one!

FEEGOBBLE:
Plead, phantom.

RINGDIVVY:
You've the floor.

HAYSEED:

From the margin of the river
(Bitter Creek, they sometimes call it)
Where I cherished once the pumpkin,
And the summer squash promoted,
Harvested the sweet potato,
Dallied with the fatal melon
And subdued the fierce cucumber,
I've been driven by the slickens,
Driven by the slimes and tailings!
All my family - my Polly
Ann and all my sons and daughters,
Dog and baby both included
All were swamped in seas of slickens,
Buried fifty fathoms under,
Where they lie, prepared to play their
Gentle prank on geologic
Gents that shall exhume them later,
In the dim and distant future,
Taking them for melancholy
Relics antedating Adam.
I alone got up and dusted.

NOZZLE:
Avaunt! you horrid and infernal cuss!
What dire distress have you prepared for us?

RINGDIVVY:
Were I a buzzard stooping from the sky
My craw with filth to fill,
Into your honorable body I
Would introduce a bill.

FEEGOBBLE:
Defendant, hence, or, by the gods, I'll brain thee!
Unless you saved some turneps to retain me.

HAYSEED:
As I was saying, I got up and dusted,
My ranch a graveyard and my business busted!
But hearing that a fellow from the City,
Who calls himself a Citizens' Committee,
Was coming up to play the very dickens,
With those who cover up our farms with slickens,
And make himself - unless I am in error
To all such miscreants a holy terror,
I thought if I would join the dialogue
I maybe might get payment for my dog.

ALL (Singing):
O the dog is the head of Creation,
Prime work of the Master's hand;

He hasn't a known occupation,
Yet lives on the fat of the land.
Adipose, indolent, sleek and orbicular,
Sun-soaken, door matted, cross and particular,
Men, women, children, all coddle and wait on him,
Then, accidentally shutting the gate on him,
Miss from their calves, ever after, the rifted out
Mouthful of tendons that doggy has lifted out!

(Enter Junket.)

JUNKET:
Well met, my hearties! I must trouble you
Jointly and severally to provide
A comfortable carriage, with relays
Of hardy horses. This Committee means
To move in state about the country here.
I shall expect at every place I stop
Good beds, of course, and everything that's nice,
With bountiful repast of meat and wine.
For this Committee comes to sea and mark
And inwardly digest.

HAYSEED:
Digest my dog!

NOZZLE:
First square my claim for damages: the gold
Escaping with the slickens keeps me poor!

RINGDIVVY:
I merely would remark that if you'd grease
My itching palm it would more glibly glide
Into the public pocket.

FEEGOBBLE:
Sir, the wheels
Of justice move but slowly till they're oiled.
I have some certain writs and warrants here,
Prepared against your advent. You recall
The tale of Zaccheus, who did climb a tree,
And Jesus said: 'Come down'?

JUNKET:
Why, bless your souls!
I've got no money; I but came to see
What all this noisy babble is about,
Make a report and file the same away.

NOZZLE, RINGDIVVY, FEEGOBBLE, HAYSEED:
How'll that help us? Reports are not our style Of provender!

JUNKET:
Well, you can gnaw the file.

Thanksgiving

The Superintendent of an Almshouse. A Pauper.

SUPERINTENDENT:
So you're unthankful - you'll not eat the bird?
You sit about the place all day and gird.
I understand you'll not attend the ball
That's to be given to-night in Pauper Hall.

PAUPER:
Why, that is true, precisely as you've heard:
I have no teeth and I will eat no bird.

SUPERINTENDENT:
Ah! see how good is Providence. Because
Of teeth He has denuded both your jaws
The fowl's made tender; you can overcome it
By suction; or at least - well, you can gum it,
Attesting thus the dictum of the preachers
That Providence is good to all His creatures
Turkeys excepted. Come, ungrateful friend,
If our Thanksgiving dinner you'll attend
You shall say grace - ask God to bless at least
The soft and liquid portions of the feast.

PAUPER.
Without those teeth my speech is rather thick
He'll hardly understand Gum Arabic.
No, I'll not dine to-day. As to the ball,
'Tis known to you that I've no legs at all.
I had the gout - hereditary; so,
As it could not be cornered in my toe
They cut my legs off in the fond belief
That shortening me would make my anguish brief.
Lacking my legs I could not prosecute
With any good advantage a pursuit;
And so, because my father chose to court
Heaven's favor with his ortolans and Port
(Thanksgiving every day!) the Lord supplied
Saws for my legs, an almshouse for my pride
And, once a year, a bird for my inside.
No, I'll not dance - my light fantastic toe
Took to its heels some twenty years ago.
Some small repairs would be required for putting

My feelings on a saltatory footing.

(Sings)
O the legless man's an unhappy chap
Tum - hi, tum - hi, tum - he o'haddy
The favors o' fortune fall not in his lap
Tum - hi, tum - heedle - do hum
The plums of office avoid his plate
No matter how much he may stump the State
Tum - hi, ho - heeee.
The grass grows never beneath his feet,
But he cannot hope to make both ends meet
Tum - hi.
With a gleeless eye and a somber heart,
He plays the role of his mortal part:
Wholly himself he can never be.
O, a soleless corporation is he!
Tum.

SUPERINTENDENT:
The chapel bell is calling, thankless friend,
Balls you may not, but church you shall, attend.
Some recognition cannot be denied
To the great mercy that has turned aside
The sword of death from us and let it fall
Upon the people's necks in Montreal;
That spared our city, steeple, roof and dome,
And drowned the Texans out of house and home;
Blessed all our continent with peace, to flood
The Balkan with a cataclysm of blood.
Compared with blessings of so high degree,
Your private woes look mighty small - to me.

The Birth Of The Rail

DRAMATIS PERSONAE
LELAND, THE KID a Road Agent
COWBOY CHARLEY Same Line of Business
HAPPY HUNTY Ditto in All Respects
SOOTYMUG a Devil

Scene - the Dutch Flat Stage Road, at 12 P.M., on a Night of 1864.

COWBOY CHARLEY:
My boss, I fear she is delayed to-night.
Already it is past the hour, and yet
My ears have reached no sound of wheels; no note
Melodious, of long, luxurious oaths
Betokens the traditional dispute

(Unsettled from the dawn of time) between
The driver and off wheeler; no clear chant
Nor carol of Wells Fargo's messenger
Unbosoming his soul upon the air
his prowess to the tender-foot,
And how at divers times in sundry ways
He strewed the roadside with our carcasses.
Clearly, the stage will not come by to-night.

LELAND, THE KID:
I now remember that but yesterday
I saw three ugly looking fellows start
From Colfax with a gun apiece, and they
Did seem on business of importance bent.
Furtively casting all their eyes about
And covering their tracks with all the care
That business men do use. I think perhaps
They were Directors of that rival line,
The great Pacific Mail. If so, they have
Indubitably taken in that coach,
And we are overreached. Three times before
This thing has happened, and if once again
These outside operators dare to cut
Our rates of profit I shall quit the road
And take my money out of this concern.
When robbery no longer pays expense
It loses then its chiefest charm for me,
And I prefer to cheat - you hear me shout!

HAPPY HUNTY:
My chief, you do but echo back my thoughts:
This competition is the death of trade.
'Tis plain (unless we wish to go to work)
Some other business we must early find.
What shall it be? The field of usefulness
Is yearly narrowing with the advance
Of wealth and population on this coast.
There's little left that any man can do
Without some other fellow stepping in
And doing it as well. If one essay
To pick a pocket he is sure to feel
(With what disgust I need not say to you)
Another hand inserted in the same.
You crack a crib at dead of night, and lo!
As you explore the dining-room for plate
You find, in session there, a graceless band
Stuffing their coats with spoons, their skins with wine.
And so it goes. Why even undertake
To salt a mine and you will find it rich
With noble specimens placed there before!

LELAND, THE KID:
And yet this line of immigration has
Advantages superior to aught
That elsewhere offers: all these passengers,
If punched with care

COWBOY CHARLEY:
Significant remark!
It opens up a prospect wide and fair,
Suggesting to the thoughtful mind - my mind
A scheme that is the boss lay-out. Instead
Of stopping passengers, let's carry them.
Instead of crying out: 'Throw up your hands!'
Let's say: 'Walk up and buy a ticket!' Why
Should we unwieldy goods and bullion take,
Watches and all such trifles, when we might
Far better charge their value three times o'er
For carrying them to market?

LELAND, THE KID:
Put it there,
Old son!

HAPPY HUNTY:
You take the cake, my dear. We'll build
A mighty railroad through this pass, and then
The stage folk will come up to us and squeal,
And say: 'It is bad medicine for both:
What will you give or take?' And then we'll sell.

COWBOY CHARLEY:
Enlarge your notions, little one; this is
No petty, slouching, opposition scheme,
To be bought off like honest men and fools;
Mine eye prophetic pierces through the mists
That cloud the future, and I seem to see
A well-devised and executed scheme
Of wholesale robbery within the law
(Made by ourselves) great, permanent, sublime,
And strong to grapple with the public throat
Shaking the stuffing from the public purse,
The tears from bankrupt merchants' eyes, the blood
From widows' famished carcasses, the bread
From orphans' mouths!

HAPPY HUNTY:
Hooray!

LELAND, THE; KID:
Hooray!

ALL:
Hooray!

(They tear the masks from their faces, and discharging their shotguns, throw them into the chapparal. Then they join hands, dance and sing the following song:)

Ah! blessed to measure
The glittering treasure!
Ah! blessed to heap up the gold
Untold
That flows in a wide
And deepening tide
Rolled, rolled, rolled
From multifold sources,
Converging its courses
Upon our -

LELAND, THE KID:
Just wait a bit, my pards, I thought I heard
A sneaking grizzly cracking the dry twigs.
Such an intrusion might deprive the State
Of all the good that we intend it. Ha!

(Enter Sootymug. He saunters carelessly in and gracefully leans his back against a redwood.)

SOOTYMUG:
My boys, I thought I heard
Some careless revelry,
As if your minds were stirred
By some new devilry.
I too am in that line. Indeed, the mission
On which I come -

HAPPY HUNTY:
Here's more damned competition!
(Curtain.)

The Brothers

Scene - A lawyer's dreadful den.

Enter stall-fed citizen.

LAWYER. 'Mornin'. How-de-do?

CITIZEN. Sir, same to you.
Called as counsel to retain you
In a case that I'll explain you.
Sad, so sad! Heart almost broke.

Hang it! where's my kerchief? Smoke?
Brother, sir, and I, of late,
Came into a large estate.
Brother's-h'm, ha, rather queer
Sometimes (tapping forehead) here.
What he needs - you know - a 'writ'
Something, eh? that will permit
Me to manage, sir, in fine,
His estate, as well as mine.
'Course he'll kick; 't will break, I fear,
His loving heart - excuse this tear.

LAWYER. Have you nothing more?
All of this you said before
When last night I took your case.

CITIZEN. Why, sir, your face
Ne'er before has met my view!

LAWYER. Eh? The devil! True:
My mistake - it was your brother.
But you're very like each other.

The Mummery

THE TWO CAVEES

DRAMATIS PERSONAE.
FITCH a Pelter of Railrogues
PICKERING his Partner, an Enemy to Sin
OLD NICK a General Blackwasher
DEAD CAT a Missile
ANTIQUE EGG Another
RAILROGUES, DUMP-CARTERS. NAVVIES and Unassorted SHOVELRY in the Lower Distance

Scene - The Brink of a Railway Cut, a Mile Deep.

Time - 1875.

FITCH:
Gods! what a steep declivity! Below
I see the lazy dump-carts come and go,
Creeping like beetles and about as big.
The delving Paddies

PICKERING:
Case of infra dig.

FITCH:

Loring, light-minded and unmeaning quips
Come with but scant propriety from lips
Fringed with the blue-black evidence of age.
'Twere well to cultivate a style more sage,
For men will fancy, hearing how you pun,
Our foulest missiles are but thrown in fun.

(Enter Dead Cat.)

Here's one that thoughtfully has come to hand;
Slant your fine eye below and see it land.

(Seizes Dead Cat by the tail and swings it in act to throw.)

DEAD CAT (singing):
Merrily, merrily, round I go
Over and under and at.
Swing wide and free, swing high and low
The anti-monopoly cat!
O, who wouldn't be in the place of me,
The anti-monopoly cat?
Designed to admonish,
Persuade and astonish
The capitalist and

FITCH (letting go):
Scat!

(Exit Dead Cat.)

PICKERING:
Huzza! good Deacon, well and truly flung!
Pat Stanford it has grassed, and Mike de Young.
Mike drives a dump-cart for the villains, though
'Twere fitter that he pull it. Well, we owe
The traitor one for leaving us! - some day
We'll get, if not his place, his cart away.
Meantime fling missiles - any kind will do.

(Enter Antique Egg.)

Ha! we can give them an ovation, too!

ANTIQUE EGG:
In the valley of the Nile,
Where the Holy Crocodile
Of immeasurable smile
Blossoms like the early rose,
And the Sacred Onion grows
When the Pyramids were new
And the Sphinx possessed a nose,

By a storkess I was laid
In the cool papyrus shade,
Where the rushes later grew,
That concealed the little Jew,
Baby Mose.
Straining very hard to hatch,
I disrupted there my yolk;
And I felt my yellow streaming
Through my white;
And the dream that I was dreaming
Of posterity was broke
In a night.
Then from the papyrus-patch
By the rising waters rolled,
Passing many a temple old,
I proceeded to the sea.
Memnon sang, one morn, to me,
And I heard Cambyses sass
The tomb of Ozymandias!

FITCH:
O, venerablest orb of all the earth,
God rest the lady fowl that gave thee birth!
Fit missile for the vilest hand to throw
I freely tender thee mine own. Although
As a bad egg I am myself no slouch,
Thy riper years thy ranker worth avouch.
Now, Pickering, please expose your eye and say If - whoop!

(Exit egg.)

I've got the range.

PICKERING:
Hooray! hooray!
A grand good shot, and Teddy Colton's down:
It burst in thunderbolts upon his crown!
Larry O'Crocker drops his pick and flies,
And deafening odors scream along the skies!
Pelt 'em some more.

FITCH:
There's nothing left but tar
wish I were a Yahoo.

PICKERING:
Well, you are.
But keep the tar. How well I recollect,
When Mike was in with us - proud, strong, erect
Mens conscia recti flinging mud, he stood,
Austerely brave, incomparably good,

Ere yet for filthy lucre he began
To drive a cart as Stanford's hired man,
That pitch-pot bearing in his hand, Old Nick
Appeared and tarred us all with the same stick.

(Enter Old Nick).

I hope he won't return and use his arts
To make us part with our immortal parts.

OLD NICK:
Make yourself easy on that score my lamb;
For both your souls I wouldn't give a damn!
I want my tar-pot - hello! where's the stick?

FITCH:
Don't look at me that fashion! - look at Pick.

PICKERING:
Forgive me, father - pity my remorse!
Truth is - Mike took that stick to spank his horse.
It fills my pericardium with grief
That I kept company with such a thief.

(Endeavoring to get his handkerchief, he opens his coat and the tar-stick falls out. Nick picks it up, looks at the culprit reproachfully and withdraws in tears.)

FITCH (excitedly):
O Pickering, come hither to the brink
There's something going on down there, I think!
With many an upward smile and meaning wink
The navvies all are running from the cut
Like lunatics, to right and left

PICKERING:
Tut, tut
'Tis only some poor sport or boisterous joke.
Let us sit down and have a quiet smoke.

(They sit and light cigars.)

FITCH (singing):
When first I met Miss Toughie
I smoked a fine cigyar,
An' I was on de dummy
And she was in de cyar.

BOTH (singing):
An' I was on de dummy
And she was in de cyar.

FITCH (singing):
I couldn't go to her,
An' she wouldn't come to me;
An' I was as oneasy
As a gander on a tree.

BOTH (singing):
An' I was as oneasy
As a gander on a tree.

FITCH (singing):
But purty soon I weakened
An' lef' de dummy's bench,
An' frew away a ten-cent weed
To win a five-cent wench!

BOTH (singing)
An' frew away a ten-cent weed
To win a five-cent wench!

FITCH:
Is there not now a certain substance sold
Under the name of fulminate of gold,
A high explosive, popular for blasting,
Producing an effect immense and lasting?

PICKERING:
Nay, that's mere superstition. Rocks are rent
And excavations made by argument.
Explosives all have had their day and season;
The modern engineer relies on reason.
He'll talk a tunnel through a mountain's flank
And by fair speech cave down the tallest bank.

(The earth trembles, a deep subterranean explosion is heard and a section of the bank as big as El Capitan starts away and plunges thunderously into the cut. A part of it strikes De Young's dumpcart abaft the axletree and flings him, hurtling, skyward, a thing of legs and arms, to descend on the distant mountains, where it is cold. Fitch and Pickering pull themselves out of the debris and stand ungraveling their eyes and noses.)

FITCH:
Well, since I'm down here I will help to grade,
And do dirt-throwing henceforth with a spade.

PICKERING:
God bless my soul! it gave me quit a start.
Well, fate is fate - I guess I'll drive this cart.

The Scurril Press

OM JONESMITH (loquitur): I've slept right through
The night - a rather clever thing to do.
How soundly women sleep (looks at his wife.)
They're all alike. The sweetest thing in life
Is woman when she lies with folded tongue,
Its toil completed and its day-song sung.
(Thump) That's the morning paper.
What a bore That it should be delivered at the door.
There ought to be some expeditious way
To get it to one. By this long delay
The fizz gets off the news (a rap is heard).
That's Jane, the housemaid; she's an early bird;
She's brought it to the bedroom door, good soul.
(Gets up and takes it in.) Upon the whole
The system's not so bad a one. What's here?
Gad, if they've not got after-listen dear
(To sleeping wife) young Gastrotheos!
Well, If Freedom shrieked when Kosciusko fell
She'll shriek again - with laughter - seeing how
They treated Gast. with her. Yet I'll allow
'T is right if he goes dining at The Pup
With Mrs. Thing.

WIFE (briskly, waking up):
With her? The hussy! Yes, it serves him right.

JONESMITH (continuing to 'seek the light'):
What's this about old Impycu? That's good!
Grip - that's the funny man - says Impy should
Be used as a decoy in shooting tramps.
I knew old Impy when he had the 'stamps'
To buy us all out, and he wasn't then
So bad a chap to have about. Grip's pen
Is just a tickler! and the world, no doubt,
Is better with it than it was without.
What? thirteen ladies - Jumping Jove! we know
Them nearly all! who gamble at a low
And very shocking game of cards called 'draw'!
O cracky, how they'll squirm! ha - ha! haw - haw!
Let's see what else (wife snores). Well, I'll be blest!
A woman doesn't understand a jest.
Hello! What, what? the scurvy wretch proceeds
To take a fling at me, condemn him! (reads):
Tom Jonesmith - my name's Thomas, vulgar cad!
Of the new Shavings Bank - the man's gone mad!
That's libelous; I'll have him up for that
Has had his corns cut. Devil take the rat!
What business is 't of his, I'd like to know?
He didn't have to cut them. Gods! what low
And scurril things our papers have become!

You skim their contents and you get but scum.
Here, Mary, (waking wife) I've been attacked
In this vile sheet. By Jove, it is a fact!

WIFE (reading it): How wicked! Who do you
Suppose 't was wrote it?

JONESMITH: Who? why, who
But Grip, the so - called funny man - he wrote
Me up because I'd not discount his note.
(Blushes like sunset at the hideous lie
He'll think of one that's better by and by
Throws down the paper on the floor, and treads
A lively measure on it - kicks the shreds
And patches all about the room, and still
Performs his jig with unabated will.)

WIFE (warbling sweetly, like an Elfland horn):
Dear, do be careful of that second corn.

STANLEY: Noting some great man's composition vile:
A head of wisdom and a heart of guile,
A will to conquer and a soul to dare,
Joined to the manners of a dancing bear,
Fools unaccustomed to the wide survey
Of various Nature's compensating sway,
Untaught to separate the wheat and chaff,
To praise the one and at the other laugh,
Yearn all in vain and impotently seek
Some flawless hero upon whom to wreak
The sycophantic worship of the weak.
Not so the wise, from superstition free,
Who find small pleasure in the bended knee;
Quick to discriminate 'twixt good and bad,
And willing in the king to find the cad
No reason seen why genius and conceit,
The power to dazzle and the will to cheat,
The love of daring and the love of gin,
Should not dwell, peaceful, in a single skin.
To such, great Stanley, you're a hero still,
Despite your cradling in a tub for swill.
Your peasant manners can't efface the mark
Of light you drew across the Land of Dark.
In you the extremes of character are wed,
To serve the quick and villify the dead.
Hero and clown! O, man of many sides,
The Muse of Truth adores you and derides,
And sheds, impartial, the revealing ray
Upon your head of gold and feet of clay.

Ambrose Bierce – A Short Biography

Ambrose Gwinnett Bierce had a diverse literary, military and journalistic career, during which his sardonic view of human nature ensured he was both frequently critical and frequently criticised. As a writer, his work included short stories, fables, editorials and his journalism, which was often controversial owing to his vehemence and acerbic style.

He was born on June 24th 1842 to Marcus Aurelius Bierce (1799-1876) and Laura Sherwood Bierce at Horse Cave Creek in Meigs Country, Ohio. Though his parents were poor they were literarily inclined and they introduced Bierce to this passion at an early age, instilling in him a deep appreciation of books, the written word and the elegance of language.

Bierce grew up in Koscuisko Country, Indiana, attending school at the county seat in Warsaw. He was the tenth of thirteen children, all of whom Marcus Aurelius gave names beginning with 'A', an indication of his love of poetry and alliteration. In order of birth they were Abigail, Amelia, Ann, Addison, Aurelius, Augustus, Almeda, Andrew, Albert, Ambrose, Arthur, Adelia and Aurelia. Poverty and religion were defining features of his childhood, and he would later describe his parents as "unwashed savages" and fanatically religious, showing him little affection but quick to punish him "with anything they could lay their hand on". He soon came to resent religion, and an introduction to literature is about the only lasting effect Marcus Aurelius had on Bierce.

Instead, Bierce began to respect his Uncle Lucius, whose "political and military distinction won the admiration of his nephew"; as an important figure within the American military and a graduate of Ohio University, he seemed far more worthy of admiration than his father. The family moved Westward when he was nine "in search of better land, and a more promising future", settling on 80 acres of farmland in Walnut Creek, Indiana.

Then, at the age of fifteen, Bierce left home to become a printer's devil, mixing ink and fetching type at The Northern Indian, a small Ohio newspaper run by a man named Reuben Williams. The duration of his time here is uncertain, though it is known that he quit the apprenticeship; apparently after being falsely accused of a theft. He returned to the family farm and spent time sending work to editors in the hopes of being published, though he was met with frequent rejection.

On the recommendation of his Uncle Lucius he was sent to the Kentucky Military Institute where, after a year's education, he was commissioned as an Officer in the Union Army. At the outset of the American Civil War in 1861, Bierce enlisted in the Union Army's 9th Indiana Infantry Regiment. His first major participation was during the Operations in Western Virginia campaign of 1861, and he was present at the 'first battle' at Philippi.

At the Battle of Rich Mountain on July 11th 1861 he executed the daring rescue of a gravely wounded comrade under heavy enemy fire, an act of bravery which received attention in the newspaper. Following this triumph he was commissioned First Lieutenant, serving as a topographical engineer on the staff of General William Babcock Hazen, undertaking the important work of making maps of likely battlefields.

In April 1862 Bierce fought at the Battle of Shiloh, an experience which, though terrifying, became the source of several of his short stories in later years, along with the memoir What I Saw of Shiloh. Two more years of valuable service followed until June 1864 when, while fighting at the Battle of Kennesaw Mountain, he sustained a serious head wound which required him to spend the summer on furlough, an unpaid yet honourable period of leave, in order to recover. He returned to active duty in September of that year, only to be discharged in January 1865 towards the close of the war.

However midway through 1866 he rejoined General Hazen on his expedition to inspect military outposts across the Great Plains, proceeding by horseback and wagon from Omaha, Nebraska, to San Francisco, California, at the end of the year.

While still in San Francisco, Bierce was presented with the rank of brevet major before tendering his resignation from the Army, choosing to remain in San Francisco and becoming involved with publishing and editing. On Christmas Day of 1871 Bierce married Mary Ellen, also known as Molly, with whom he had his first child, Day, the following year.

Later in 1872 he moved to England where he lived and wrote between the years 1872 and 1875, contributing work to Fun magazine. In 1874 his second son, Leigh, was born, and while in England he saw his first book, The Fiend's Delight, published by John Camden Hotton under the pseudonym 'Dod Grile'. It appeared in London in 1873, and was a collection of his articles. On the back of this success he was published twice more, first Nuggets and Dust Panned Out in California in 1873, and the next year Cobwebs from and Empty Skull, both collections of stories, fables, maxims, sketches, poetry, epigrams, quips and witticisms.

After this success and his continued regular contribution to Fun, he returned to San Francisco where he took up a more permanent residence and focused on his editorial career, working for a number of local papers including The San Francisco News Letter, The Argonaut, the Overland Monthly, The Californian and The Wasp. His crime writing was some of the finest of the medium and was reproduced in the Library of America anthology True Crime. His novella 'The Dance of Death', co-written with Thomas A. Harcourth for which he used the pseudonym William Herman was published in 1877, and then from 1879 to 1880 he travelled to the Dakota Territory, visiting Rockerville and Deadwood and experimenting with a managerial role at a New York mining company.

With the failure of that company he returned to San Francisco to continue his journalism, where in 1887 he began a column at the San Francisco Examiner named 'Prattle', which saw him become one of William Randolph Hearst's first regular columnists and editors at the paper. He eventually became one of the more influential and prominent of the journalists and writers of the West Coast. His association with Hearst Newspapers would continue until 1906.

Bierce's marriage was to fall apart when in 1888 he discovered compromising letters to his wife from a secret admirer. This led to their separation. The following year, 1889 his first son Day committed suicide following depression brought on by a romantic rejection.

In 1891, inspired by his time in the Union Army, Bierce wrote and published the collection of 26 short stories, Tales of Soldiers and Civilians which included his famous 'An Occurrence at Owl Creek Bridge'. Maintaining in the preface to the first edition that the book had been "denied existence by the chief publishing houses in the country", the eventual publication is accredited to his friend Mr E.L.G. Steele, a San Franciscan merchant against whose name the 1891 copyright is listed. The heavy irony of his depictions of battlefield heroism and valour perhaps reflects his own response to the differences between his act of human bravery, rescuing a comrade, and the 'brave sacrifices' of troop leaders whose stubborn and rash decisions often led to the deaths of many whose lives could have been spared by more prudent warmongering. A particular example of this is found in the actions of Lieutenant Brayle, of the story 'Incident at Resaca', in whose orders for a hundred men to charge gloriously into certain death Bierce presents valourous sacrifice, ideally rendered, but it is a portrayal which he then juxtaposes against the gruesomely realistic descriptions of their wounds and deaths. Moreover, alongside these informed accounts of battlefield brutality he acknowledges the frequent injuries sustained by women and children which were oft overlooked by official accounts and propaganda.

Three more publications followed, a book of poetry in 1892 entitled Black Beetles in Amber, followed by a novella, again co-written but this time with Adolphe De Castro named The Monk and the Hangman's Daughter, also published in 1892 and Can Such Things Be?, a collection of short stories which reached print in 1893. By this time the Union Pacific and Central Pacific railroad companies were receiving huge loans from the United States Government towards their endeavours to build the First Transcontinental Railroad, and Collis P. Huntingdon sought to introduce a bill which quietly excused the companies from repaying the money, essentially converting the loan into a handout of $130 million dollars. The plot's essence was secrecy, for its perpetrators hoped to get the bill through Congress without any public notice and subsequent hearing, so in 1896 Hearst dispatched Bierce to Washington, D.C to scupper their plans. Confronted by Huntingdon on the steps of the Capitol and angrily invited to name his price, Bierce answered "my price is $130 million dollars. If, when you are ready to pay, I happen to be out of town, you may hand it over to my friend, the Treasurer of the United States". This answer became famous and was recorded in newspapers nationwide, and his coverage of and diatribes on the issue encouraged such public outrage that the bill was challenged and defeated. Following this huge success, Bierce returned to California in November.

He now began his first foray into a career as a fabulist, publishing Fantastic Fables in 1899 and anticipating the rise of ironic grotesquerie which was seen in the 20th century. The following year, owing to his penchant for stirring up the public through his biting satire and social criticism, he induced a hostile reaction to a poem he had written in 1900 about the assassination of Governor Goebel and following the assassination of President William McKinley which had been deliberately misconstrued by Hearst's opponents, turning it into something of a cause célèbre. The poem was meant to express the national sense of fear and dismay at Goebel's death, but the lines

> The bullet that pierced Goebel's breast
> Can not be found in all the West;
> Good reason, it is speeding here
> To stretch McKinley on his bier

(written innoculously in 1900) seemed to foreshadow the subsequent shooting on McKinley in 1901. This saw Hearst accused of having called for McKinley's assassination by his rivals and then by Elihu Root, then Secretary of State, though despite the national uproar which ended Hearst's ambitions for presidency, Bierce was never revealed as the author of the poem; nor, indeed, did Hearst ever fire him from the paper.

In 1901, his second son Leigh died of pneumonia relating to his alcoholism.

His enduring career at the paper was accompanied by several more publications, the next of which was Shapes of Clay in 1903, a book of poetry and the first publication of one of his most famous works, The Devil's Dictionary, which began life as an occasional newspaper item of satirical definitions of English words and then, in 1906, was published as a collection in book form under the name The Cynic's Word Book. In 1909 The Cynic's Word Book was reprinted under its current name, which Bierce himself preferred, as the entirety of the seventh volume of his Collected Works which brought together the majority of his short stories and poems. The same year he wrote Write it Right, a non-fiction work of literary criticism and commentary, which appeared alongside The Shadow on the Dial, and other essays. However, despite this professional success he finally divorced his wife in 1904, and she died the following year.

At the age of 71, in 1913 Bierce departed from Washington, D.C., for a tour of the battlefields upon which he had fought during the civil war. He had passed through Louisiana and Texas by December and was crossing into by way of El Paso into Mexico which was itself in the throes of revolution. He joined Pancho Villa's army as an observer in Ciudad Juárez during which time he witnessed the battle of Tierra Blanca. It is known that he accompanied Villa's army as far as the city of Chihuahua where he wrote his last known communication in the form of a letter to Blanche Partington, one of his close friends, dated 26th December 1913. He closed the letter with the words "as to me, I leave here tomorrow for an unknown destination" and then vanished without trace in what would become one of the most famous unexplained disappearances in American history. Various suggestions have been posited, including that belonging to the oral tradition of Sierra Mojada, Coahuila, which holds that Bierce was executed by firing squad in the town cemetery there. All that is known is that, by this time, he was suffering considerably from the asthma which had dogged him throughout his life and was compounded by his war injuries.

In 1920, three of his stories A Horseman in the Sky, A Watcher by the Dead and The Man and the Snake were published posthumously, and further poetry was published in 1980 under the title A Vision of Doom: Poems by Ambrose Pierce. As a writer, he often found himself splitting opinion and continues to do so in death, his writing variously described as cheap and vulgar, and conversely the best writing on war and that of a flawless American genius. Regardless of how differently his critics speak of him, his legacy is one of concise, acerbic and cruelly satirical social commentary, an authorial style of economy, fruitful observation and as a judicious wordsmith.